ITALIAN DRAWINGS

IN THE ART MUSEUM

PRINCETON UNIVERSITY

Kurt Weitzmann

Italian Drawings
in the Art Museum
Princeton University

106 SELECTED EXAMPLES

THE ART MUSEUM

PRINCETON UNIVERSITY

CONTENTS

FOREWORD

IT IS A HAPPY OCCASION for The Art Museum of Princeton University to be able to share a selection of its finest drawings in the Italian field with a larger public. Seldom seen previously, it is our hope that they will prove to be a delight to the eye on their first major excursion into the outside world since becoming a part of the collections of The Art Museum. Previously known only to international scholars and amateurs of drawings, this fine collection has enjoyed too small a public in the past. We hope that this exhibition will do much to stimulate a greater audience to investigate the resources of Princeton's collections.

I regret that Frank Jewett Mather, Jr., and Dan Fellows Platt, the major donors, could not have lived to read this publication and to see their cherished possessions presented in important exhibitions in New York and other centers remote from Princeton. Their joy was sharing their enthusiasm with students, peers, and interested laymen, and they would have been happy. This is what they hoped for in leaving to Princeton possessions that represented so much of their inner spirit.

It is a pleasure to acknowledge the gratitude of Princeton University to the late James J. Rorimer, Director of The Metropolitan Museum of Art, for his kindness in offering a haven for The Art Museum's collections of drawings during the two-year period while a new building was being constructed, and to Mr. Jacob Bean who cared for them during this time.

I should like to express my warmest congratulations to Mr. Bean for his scholarly text for the catalogue, and indicate my admiration for the skillful manner in which he conceived the exhibition, chose the drawings, and assembled the documentation. He and his staff have also taken on the burden of editing the manuscript.

In Princeton, we are especially indebted to Professor David R. Coffin, Chairman of the Department of Art and Archaeology, and to professors

7

Rensselaer W. Lee and Donald D. Egbert, members of the Publications Committee, which made the publication of the catalogue financially possible.

I can only reinforce Mr. Bean's appreciation of the members of his staff in New York, and of mine in Princeton, who did so much to bring this publication and exhibition to fruition.

It is my ultimate hope that the wide public, to which we present the exhibition, will share our pride in and love of these drawings. They do, after all, belong to all of us as a common heritage.

PATRICK J. KELLEHER
Director, The Art Museum
Princeton University

INTRODUCTION

ITALIAN DRAWINGS hold a place of honor in the Museum at Princeton University. In sheer number they overshadow drawings of other European schools, accounting for nearly half of a group of about twenty-five hundred; in interest and quality, too, they dominate the collection. Of fairly recent formation, Princeton's collection of drawings reflects the taste and commemorates the generosity of two donors, Frank Jewett Mather, Jr., and Dan Fellows Platt. The pre-eminence of Italian draughtsmanship at Princeton is due above all to Platt, who bequeathed to the University more than seven hundred drawings of the Italian school. Platt, Princeton class of 1895, became interested in Italian art as an undergraduate. Jurisprudence was his vocation, but the study and the collecting of Italian works of art were his passionate avocations. Throughout his long life he traveled extensively, and one of his early Italian tours is recorded in an amusing travelogue, *Through Italy with Car and Camera*, published in 1908. Like so many English and American *amateurs* of his generation, he was first drawn to Italian painting of the fourteenth and fifteenth centuries. He coveted, and was fortunate enough to obtain, some of those gold-ground panels that had been reverently rediscovered by pioneering scholars and collectors in the second half of the nineteenth century. But by the end of the First World War supply was hopelessly outdistanced by demand in this, his favorite field, and Platt, by then an inveterate collector, intelligently turned his attention to another domain. In the 1920s he discovered that fine Italian drawings of the seventeenth and eighteenth centuries, then rather neglected in favor of earlier, more Berensonian periods, could be found on the London market in great numbers. Remarkable groups of drawings by Guercino, Salvator Rosa, and both Giambattista and Domenico Tiepolo were available at prices that seem unbelievable today, when all four of these draughtsmen, par-

9

ticularly the latter two, have rocketed to the summit of international fashion. Platt bought with lavish discrimination in this buyer's market, and in his bequest Princeton University received the lion's share of these exceptional groups. A wide selection from these forward-looking acquisitions is included in the present exhibition. Nine drawings by Rosa are included, chosen from a group of more than thirty by this brilliant draughtsman, the largest representation in any American collection. Guercino is richly accounted for, with sixteen drawings from the large group that Platt bequeathed. The series of Giambattista Tiepolo's figure drawings is very fine, thanks to his purchases of sheets from two albums of Giambattista's drawings, contemporary volumes inscribed *Sole Figure per Soffitti* and *Sole Figure Vestite*, which were broken up in London in the 1920s. Other exceptional Giambattista and Domenico drawings came from different sources, and reveal Platt's intention to build up as complete as possible a representation of the work of father and son. Platt was by no means exclusively interested in the seventeenth and eighteenth centuries; the chalk studies by Barocci (nos. 13–15), the two tempera heads by Beccafumi (nos. 3, 4), and the two monumental Naldini copies after Michelangelo (nos. 19, 20) show him as an excellent judge of sixteenth-century draughtsmanship.

The other founding benefactor of the Princeton collection was Frank Jewett Mather, Jr., Professor of Fine Arts at Princeton from 1910 to 1933. Mather had the interests of the Princeton Museum's collection at heart in much the same way as his contemporary Professor Paul J. Sachs at Harvard. Professor Mather began his collecting early, at a time when an imaginative and experienced eye could find much for very little. By 1930 his collection of drawings was exhibited at the Roerich Museum in New York, and almost all the drawings later given by him to Princeton and included in the present exhibition were in his possession at that time. Mather's interests as a collector of Italian drawings were wide, ranging from the early North Italian Coronation of the Virgin attributed to the circle of

Altichiero (no. 1) to the Giambattista Tiepolo figure study from the Clerici series (no. 78). One drawing in this exhibition is a recent gift of Margaret Mower (no. 28), two were presented by Nathan V. Hammer (nos. 70, 96), while sheets by Cantagallina (no. 32), Gaulli (no. 69), and G. B. Tiepolo (no. 95) have been chosen from purchases made in the past decade by The Art Museum, some of them with funds left by Professor Clifton Hall in memory of his mother, Laura P. Hall. They reflect the Museum's resolve to enrich the important nucleus of Italian drawings, the Princeton collection having been intended since its inception to be primarily a teaching instrument and to provide source material for the Department of Art and Archaeology. However, the beauty of the Italian drawings at Princeton transcends this estimable academic function.

During the construction in 1964–1965 of the new Art Museum at Princeton, its collection of drawings was deposited at The Metropolitan Museum of Art, and at that time the present selection was made and this brief but fully illustrated catalogue prepared. The whole collection will in due course be installed in a new Print Room at Princeton, adjacent to an exhibition gallery designed especially for drawings and prints. The interim period seemed a particularly suitable occasion to prepare a traveling exhibition of Italian drawings, one that would give the public elsewhere the opportunity to judge and appreciate Princeton's exceptional resources.

These resources, surprisingly enough, are little known. Some drawings, the Mather Carpaccio, the Platt Baroccis, and the Domenico Tintorettos, for example, figure in the standard literature, but a great many of the drawings in the catalogue have not hitherto been published, and have never been exhibited outside Princeton. The exceptional series of Guercinos is almost unknown, having been listed only in Mrs. Lynes's unpublished thesis on the drawings by this artist in the Platt collection. The same is true of the Rosa drawings, though Michael Mahoney has recently discussed them in his unpublished thesis on Rosa as a draughtsman, an important study that he has kindly made available to this author. The only complete publication of a group of drawings at Princeton is George Knox's excellent article on the Giambattista and Domenico Tiepolo drawings, the subject of one number of the *Record of The Art Museum*, a periodical publication in which individual Princeton drawings have occasionally been studied by members of the University faculty.

The drawings have been arranged in chronological order, the date or approximate date of the artist's birth determining his place in the sequence. The bibliography under each entry contains essential published references to the drawing; exhibitions cited have been limited to those commemorated by a descriptive catalogue.

The author would like to express his gratitude to Denis Mahon, who has supplied much information concerning the Guercino drawings. Linda Lee Boyer, Pamela Osborn McVeigh, and Anne MacDougall Preuss of The Metropolitan Museum of Art have been of great assistance in the preparation of the catalogue. Patrick J. Kelleher, Director, Frances Follin Jones, and Hedy Backlin-Landman, of The Art Museum, and Felton Gibbons, of the Department of Art and Archaeology, Princeton University, have all been most helpful.

JACOB BEAN
Curator of Drawings
The Metropolitan Museum of Art

REFERENCES

WORKS CITED IN AN ABBREVIATED FORM

BENESCH, *Venetian Drawings*
> Otto Benesch, *Venetian Drawings of the Eighteenth Century in America*, New York, 1947.

KNOX, *Princeton Record*, 1964
> George Knox, "Drawings by Giambattista and Domenico Tiepolo at Princeton," *Record of The Art Museum. Princeton University*, XXIII, no. 1, 1964, pp. 2–28.

LUGT
> Frits Lugt, *Les Marques de collections de dessins et d'estampes . . .*, Amsterdam, 1921; *Supplément*, The Hague, 1956.

LYNES, *Platt Guercino Drawings*
> Mildred Aiken Lynes, "The Drawings of Guercino in the Dan Fellows Platt Collection; Englewood, New Jersey. Submitted in partial fulfillment of the requirements for the degree of Master of Arts at New York University, Institute of Fine Arts," 1940. Unpublished.

MAHONEY, *Rosa Drawings*
> Michael Mahoney, "The Drawings of Salvator Rosa. Submitted in 1965 as a Doctoral Thesis to the Courtauld Institute of Art, University of London." Unpublished.

MRAS, *Princeton Record*, 1956
> George P. Mras, "Some Drawings by G. B. Tiepolo," *Record of The Art Museum. Princeton University*, XV, no. 2, 1956, pp. 39–59.

BYAM SHAW, *Domenico Tiepolo*
> J. Byam Shaw, *The Drawings of Domenico Tiepolo*, London, 1962.

TIETZE, *Venetian Drawings*
> Hans Tietze and E. Tietze-Conrat, *The Drawings of the Venetian Painters in the 15th and 16th Centuries*, New York, 1944.

EXHIBITIONS CITED IN AN ABBREVIATED FORM

New York, Roerich Museum, 1930
> New York, International Art Center of Roerich Museum, Exhibition of Drawings by Old Masters from the Private Collection of Frank Jewett Mather, Jr., 1930.

Staten Island, Italian Drawings and Sculpture, 1958–1959
> Staten Island, Staten Island Museum, Italian Drawings and Sculpture from the Renaissance to the Present, 1958–1959.

CATALOGUE

ALTICHIERO, Circle of
Veronese or Paduan, end of the fourteenth century

1   *The Coronation of the Virgin*

Pen and brown ink, brown and rose wash, heightened with white. 6 3/8 × 7 1/2 inches (16.2 × 19 cm.). Considerable losses at lower margin, where sheet is cut irregularly.

Verso: Cavalier on a galloping horse. Pen and brown ink, brown and rose wash, heightened with white. The old mount covers part of the verso, and reveals a surface measuring only 3 3/4 × 5 9/16 inches (9.5 × 14.2 cm.).

When Borenius published this drawing in 1927, it was fixed to a mount that bore on the reverse an inscription, said to be in Padre Resta's hand, connecting the drawing with the Giottesque altarpiece in the Baroncelli Chapel of S. Croce, Florence, a claim that was rightly contradicted in a note by Jonathan Richardson Junior or Senior. Borenius pointed out the North Italian complexity of the architectural setting for this Coronation of the Virgin, suggesting affinities with polyptychs of the Vivarini school. Earlier North Italian examples should be cited: there are striking points of contact, especially in the architectural background, with Altichiero's Coronation in the Cappella Dotto of the Eremitani at Padua and his Coronation of the Virgin in the Oratorio di S. Giorgio, Padua. No authenticated drawings by Altichiero seem to have survived, and it would be hazardous to attribute this rare sheet to Altichiero himself. Nonetheless, it shows the marked influence of his style as a painter, and it may be the

work of an artist of his circle. Dr. Annegrit Schmitt has informed the author that she and Dr. Bernhard Degenhart, who are preparing a *corpus* of early Italian drawings, consider the present sheet to be Veronese, late fourteenth century, reflecting the influence of Turone and Altichiero, an attribution in harmony with that suggested here.

PROVENANCE: Padre Resta (?); Jonathan Richardson Senior (Lugt 2184); Dr. C. D. Ginsburg (Lugt 1145); H. C. Levis, London; Frank Jewett Mather, Jr.

BIBLIOGRAPHY: Tancred Borenius, *Old Master Drawings*, I, no. 4, March 1927, p. 49, pl. 57 (as North Italian, c. 1450).

Gift of Frank Jewett Mather, Jr., 45–1

VITTORE CARPACCIO
Venice 1460/1465 – Venice about 1526

2   *Two Standing Female Figures*

VERSO:
Head of a Man and Head of a Lion

Brush, brown wash, heightened with white, over black chalk, on brownish paper. 8 15/16 × 4 11/16 inches (22.7 × 11.7 cm.).

The drawings on the recto and verso of this sheet are related, in ways difficult to define exactly, to three different pictures by Carpaccio. The recto (presumably treated as the verso by Professor Mather, who marked with his stamp the side that represents the head of a man and a lion's head) bears studies of two women in oriental costume. The Tietzes connected these with two female figures at the extreme left in the Triumph of St. George in the Scuola di S. Giorgio, Venice, datable in the first decade of the sixteenth century (repr. Lauts, pl. 112). These two figures seem to be derived from a woodcut illustration by Erhard Reuwich for Breidenbach's description of a journey to the Holy Land, *Peregrinatio in terram sanctam*, published in Mainz in 1486. In Carpaccio's composition drawing in the Uffizi for the Triumph of St. George (repr. Lauts, pl. 111) the figures appear almost exactly as they do in Reuwich's woodcut. In the Princeton drawing, however, the figure at the left differs in one detail: over a light indication of the flat circular headdress that appears in the print the artist has brushed in a high cylindrical hat. In the picture the headdress was changed again, and became a bunlike turban. The Tietzes contended that both Reuwich and Carpaccio borrowed these figures from Gentile Bellini, basing their argument on the occurrence in an Adoration of the Magi in the National Gallery, London (no. 3098, repr. Lauts, pl. IIa) of a number of motifs that reappear in Carpaccio's pictures. The Tietzes, however, held that the National Gallery Adoration was by Gentile, while more recent criticism has given it to Carpaccio himself. Lauts contends, rather more simply, that the two oriental female figures were copied by Carpaccio from the Reuwich woodcut, and the changes observable from the Uffizi composition drawing through the Princeton sheet to the finished picture seem to bear out his argument.

The fine male head on the verso was connected by the Tietzes with a figure in one of the scenes in the St. Ursula cycle now in the Venice Academy, the Engaged Couple Saying Farewell, dated 1495 (repr. Lauts, pl. 26), and the similarity is indeed striking. The lion's head was used much later, as the Tietzes pointed out, in the large canvas representing the Lion of St. Mark, signed and dated 1516, in the Ducal Palace (repr. Lauts, pl. 188).

The crisp, intelligent brushwork of the Princeton sheet has led most critics to give the drawing to Carpaccio. The only exception appears to be Pignatti, who feels that the drawing shows "unmistakable weaknesses," and goes on to argue that the occurrence on a single sheet of motifs related to three pictures of quite different dates suggests that the sheet must be a studio production, the work of some assistant presumably copying pictures and drawings at random. But the fact that studies for pictures of different dates appear on the same sheet is not conclusive evidence. On a sheet in the Gathorne-Hardy collection (Lauts, no. 8), accepted by Pignatti as well as Lauts, occur studies connectible with pictures dating from 1491 on the one hand and 1510 on the other. The artist simply used an earlier idea at a later date. The quality of the Princeton sheet, particularly the very sensitive notations of the male head on the verso, seems to justify an attribution to Carpaccio himself, and there is no reason to remove it from the rather limited corpus of his surviving drawings.

PROVENANCE: Arthur Frothingham; Guastalla (according to the Tietzes); Frank Jewett Mather, Jr. (Lugt 1853a).

BIBLIOGRAPHY: Tietze, *Venetian Drawings*, no. 640, recto repr. pl. XV, verso pl. XXIII,2; *Record of the Art Museum. Princeton University*, XIII, no. 1, 1954, recto repr. p. 13, verso repr. p. 12; Jan Lauts, *Carpaccio. Paintings and Drawings*, London, 1962, p. 276, no. 46, recto repr. pl. 119, verso repr. pl. 31; Tersio Pignatti, review of

Jan Lauts's *Carpaccio*, in *Master Drawings*, I, no. 4, 1963, p. 53.

EXHIBITIONS: New London, Lyman Allyn Museum, Fourth Anniversary Exhibition, 1936, no. 16; Montreal, The Montreal Museum of Fine Arts, Five Centuries of Drawings, 1953, no. 18, recto repr.; Newark, The Newark Museum, Old Master Drawings, 1960, no. 7, recto and verso repr.; Venice, Palazzo Ducale, Vittore Carpaccio, 1963, no. 8 of drawings catalogue, recto and verso repr.

Gift of Frank Jewett Mather, Jr., 44–274

DOMENICO BECCAFUMI
Near Siena 1486(?) – Siena 1551

3 *Head of a Woman*

Tempera and emulsion. $8\frac{15}{16} \times 6\frac{3}{8}$ inches (22.7 × 16.2 cm.). Repaired losses at upper right and at center of lower margin. Vertical and horizontal creases. Lined.

Beccafumi was in the habit of making preparatory sketches in tempera for heads and figures that appear in his pictures. Thirteen of these tempera sketches may be connected with the artist's ceiling decoration in the Sala del Concistoro in the Palazzo Pubblico in Siena, painted between 1529 and 1535. Sanminiatelli points out that the present drawing was probably used for the head of a young woman who appears in a group of figures at the left in a rectangular composition in the Concistoro ceiling, representing Posthumius Tubertus killing his own son for breach of military discipline. In addition to no. 4 below, tempera sketches for the Palazzo Pubblico ceiling, which recount stories of Greek and Roman heroism, are to be found in the Morgan Library, the Fogg Museum, the Rijksmuseum in Amsterdam, at Wiesbaden, London, and in a New York private collection.

PROVENANCE: Charles Fairfax Murray (according to inscription on mount); Dan Fellows Platt (Lugt 750a), purchased by Platt from Meatyard in 1922.

BIBLIOGRAPHY: J. Judey, "Beccafumi," inaugural dissertation, Albert-Ludwigs-Universität, Freiburg im Breisgau, 1932, p. 149, no. 229; Agnes Mongan and Paul J. Sachs, *Drawings in the Fogg Museum of Art*, I, Cambridge, Massachusetts, 1940, p. 54; Donato Sanminiatelli, "The Sketches of Domenico Beccafumi," *Burlington Magazine*, XCVII, 1955, p. 36, fig. 5.

Bequest of Dan Fellows Platt, 48–607

4 *Head of a Putto*

Tempera and emulsion. $8\frac{1}{8} \times 6\frac{13}{16}$ inches (20.6 × 17.3 cm.). Lined.

Sanminiatelli suggests that this is Beccafumi's design for the head of a putto that appears at the right of the allegorical figure of Mutual Benevolence in an octagonal compartment of the ceiling of the Sala del Concistoro in the Palazzo Pubblico at Siena. See no. 3 above.

PROVENANCE: Charles Fairfax Murray (according to inscription on mount); William Bateson (according to inscription on mount); Dan Fellows Platt (Lugt 750a), purchased by Platt from Meatyard in 1929.

BIBLIOGRAPHY: J. Judey, "Beccafumi," inaugural dissertation, Albert-Ludwigs-Universität, Freiburg im Breisgau, 1932, p. 149, no. 228; Agnes Mongan and Paul

J. Sachs, *Drawings in the Fogg Museum of Art*, I, Cambridge, Massachusetts, 1940, p. 54; Donato Sanminiatelli, "The Sketches of Domenico Beccafumi," *Burlington Magazine*, XCVII, 1955, p. 36.

EXHIBITIONS: Newark, The Newark Museum, Old Master Drawings, 1960, no. 9, repr.

Bequest of Dan Fellows Platt, 48–606

5 *Scene from the Life of St. Anthony Abbot*

Pen and brown ink, gray wash, heightened with white, on brown-washed paper. 7 1/8 × 9 1/8 inches (18.1 × 23.2 cm.). Surface considerably abraded. Upper right and left corners trimmed. Lined.

This scene from the life of St. Anthony Abbot, who stands on the left, identified by his crutch with a bell hanging from it, cannot be related to any known painted work by Beccafumi. The draughtsmanship is certainly his and in the style of his maturity; perhaps the composition is intended for a predella panel.

PROVENANCE: Unidentified collector (Lugt 2914a); Peter Lely (Lugt 2092); Jonathan Richardson Senior (Lugt 2183); Sir Joshua Reynolds (Lugt 2364); John Barnard (Lugt 1419); Dan Fellows Platt (Lugt 2066b and 750a), purchased by Platt from Meatyard in 1922.

Bequest of Dan Fellows Platt, 48–608

RAPHAEL, School of
Early sixteenth century

6 *A Papal Audience*

Pen and brown ink, brown wash, heightened with white, over red chalk, on brownish paper. 15 5/16 × 20 7/8 inches (38.9 × 53.1 cm.). Vertical crease at center, horizontal crease above center. Surface considerably abraded. Stain at lower center.

Inscribed in pen and brown ink on verso, *R. Urbino 20.3.*

Verso: Study of machinery in pen and brown ink, and anatomical studies of legs in red chalk. Most of the verso covered with an old support.

Drawings in the British Museum (Pouncey and Gere, no. 281*) and the Albertina (S. R. 296) record this composition, very probably conceived by Raphael. None of the three versions, though they are all old, can convincingly be claimed as the work of Raphael himself, but the design has an unmistakably Raphaelesque authority and is no doubt based on a lost drawing by the master. To Pouncey and Gere the style of the composition indicates a date not later than the Stanza della Segnatura (about 1510); they also point out that the grouping of the figures and their relationship to the architectural setting reveal Raphael's knowledge of the bronze reliefs by Donatello in the Santo at Padua.

The subject represented, a pope reading from an open book with a kneeling prelate before him, cannot be connected with any of Raphael's known projects for the Vatican (it does not seem to be the Coronation of Charlemagne, as Professor Mather had suggested). For Mather, who owned and first published this interesting sheet and generously left it to Princeton, the drawing was the work of Raphael himself "except the final touching in of the whites." The Albertina version has been variously attributed to Bagnacavallo, to

Perino del Vaga, and more recently to Giovanni Francesco Penni (to whom John Shearman has recently ascribed the compositional invention itself—*Burlington Magazine*, CVII, 1965, p. 35); Pouncey and Gere suggest the name of Battista Franco for the British Museum copy. The Princeton drawing is of good quality, has an excellent provenance, and differs from the two other versions in having a red chalk underdrawing. It is an intriguing Raphael school production, difficult if not impossible to attribute to a specific pupil or imitator who may have had access to Raphael's original design. Nor are the slight studies of anatomy and of machinery on the verso in an identifiable hand.

PROVENANCE: Peter Lely (Lugt 2092); Prosper Henry Lankrink (Lugt 2090); Frank Jewett Mather, Jr. (Lugt 1853a).

BIBLIOGRAPHY: Frank Jewett Mather, Jr., "An Unrecognized Composition by Raphael," *The Art Bulletin*, XII, 1930, pp. 5–10, recto repr. fig. 1, verso repr. figs. 3 and 4; Philip Pouncey and J. A. Gere, *Italian Drawings in the Department of Prints and Drawings in the British Museum. Raphael and His Circle*, I, London, 1962, pp. 169–170.

Gift of Frank Jewett Mather, Jr., 51–110

GIULIO ROMANO
Rome 1499 – Mantua 1546

7   *Man Beating a Snarling Dog*

Pen and brown ink, brown wash, on gray-washed paper. $9\frac{13}{16} \times 6\frac{5}{16}$ inches (24.9 × 16 cm.). Surface considerably abraded. Lined.

Inscribed in pen and brown ink on verso, *Iulio Romano.*

This is a typical example of Giulio's invention, in the rather savage vein so characteristic of him. Frederick Hartt did not include this drawing in his monumental work on Giulio Romano (New Haven, 1958), but the sheet, though damaged, is surely autograph.

PROVENANCE: Frank Jewett Mather, Jr.

EXHIBITIONS: Staten Island, Italian Drawings and Sculpture, 1958–1959, no. 10.

Gift of Frank Jewett Mather, Jr., 52–174

PIERO BUONACCORSI, called PERINO DEL VAGA, Studio of
Florence 1501 – Rome 1547

8   *Kneeling Figure of Mercury*

Pen and brown ink, brown wash, heightened with yellow, on paper washed in mustard brown. $15\frac{9}{16} \times 11\frac{5}{16}$ inches (39.5 ×28.7 cm.). Paper much creased. Losses at upper left and right margin. Lined.

J. A. Gere was the first to point out the connection of this drawing, formerly classed among the anonymous Italian material, with large designs in the Louvre (Anonymous Italian, Inv. 10,369, and 10,413; the Perinesque character of these two drawings was recognized by Pouncey) and at Munich (Inv. 2542 and 2543, as Perino). Like the Princeton sheet, these coarsely drawn productions, washed in mustard brown and heightened with yellow, represent mythological subjects involving Mercury, in a friezelike format that suggests they may have been projects for a monochrome façade decoration. The figures have a distinctly Perinesque air; the drawings, interesting as records, may derive from a design by Perino himself, and they may be small-scale *modelli* worked up in Perino's studio by an assistant. An additional drawing from the series, with figures of Jupiter and Diana, recently appeared in the New York market.

PROVENANCE: Count Gelozzi (Lugt 545); Frank Jewett Mather, Jr. (Lugt 1853a).

Gift of Frank Jewett Mather, Jr., 48–1791

FRANCESCO MAZZOLA, called PARMIGIANINO

Parma 1503 – Casalmaggiore 1540

9 *Seated Figure with Goats*

Red chalk. $6\frac{15}{16} \times 5\frac{1}{16}$ inches (17.7 × 12.9 cm.).

Inscribed in pen and brown ink on verso, *n° 63*.

Verso: Reclining nude female and half figure of woman in a dress with puffed sleeves.

The subject is unclear; is the seated girl (or androgynous youth) a goat-herd? Popham, who dates this drawing quite early, before Parmigianino's departure for Rome about 1524, suggests that in spite of the presence of the goats the figure might be a study for a penitent Magdalene. The reclining female nude and the half figure of a woman in a dress with puffed sleeves on the verso cannot be connected with a painted work. The verso was published by Professor Mather in 1940 as Pordenone, and the sheet was entered in the Princeton inventory under that name. However, it is an unquestionable and very attractive example of Parmigianino's draughtsmanship.

PROVENANCE: Jonathan Richardson Senior (Lugt 2183); unidentified collector's mark not described by Lugt, small six-pointed star stamped in black ink in upper left corner of recto; Duke of Rutland (according to Mather); Frank Jewett Mather, Jr.

BIBLIOGRAPHY: Frank Jewett Mather, Jr., review of Giuseppe Fiocco's *Giovanni Antonio Pordenone* in *Art in America*, XXVIII, 1940, p. 84, verso repr. p. 87 (as Pordenone); Tietze, *Venetian Drawings*, no. A1359 (the attribution to Pordenone not accepted).

Gift of Frank Jewett Mather, Jr., 48–1918

LELIO ORSI

Novellara, probably 1511 – Novellara 1587

10 *Project for the Decoration of a Façade*

Pen and brown ink, yellow-brown wash, on brown-washed paper. $9\frac{3}{8} \times 12\frac{1}{2}$ inches (23.8 × 31.8 cm.).

Inscribed in pen and brown ink at lower left, *Lelio de Novelare*.

Two other versions of this façade project have survived: one at Chatsworth (repr. *Old Master Drawings from Chatsworth*, catalogue of an exhibition circulated by the Smithsonian Institution, 1962–1963, no. 40), another at Modena in the Galleria Estense (repr. *Mostra di Lelio Orsi*, Reggio Emilia, 1950, p. 113, fig. 14). The three drawings, each distinguished by slight variations, are of comparable quality; they may well all be by Orsi himself, who according to Florence Kossoff was in the habit of repeating his own drawings. This question is complicated by Mariette's mention of what might appear to have been yet another drawing by Orsi for the same façade, seen by Mariette in Crozat's collection (*Abecedario de P. J. Mariette*, edited by Ph. de Chennevières and A. de Montaiglon, IV, Paris, 1857–1858, p. 64). The Princeton sheet, however, bears the paraph of the seventeenth-century French collector Desneux de la Noue; Crozat obtained a number of drawings from the heirs of Desneux, and the Princeton project may well have been the one recorded by Mariette. Popham has pointed out that the coat of arms at the top center of the design, representing two bears (*orsi*) confronted, is that of the artist himself. The project thus could be a scheme for the exterior decoration of Orsi's own house. The figure of the crossbowman at the lower center of the design is studied in a wash drawing at Windsor (repr. A. E. Popham and J. Wilde, *The Italian Drawings of the XV and XVI Centuries . . . at Windsor Castle*, London, 1949, no. 529, pl. 134).

PROVENANCE: Desneux de la Noue (Lugt 3014); Pierre Crozat (?); Sir John Charles Robinson (Lugt 1433; inscribed in pencil on old mat, *Lelio Orsi da Novellara. This drawing was for the fresco decoration of the front of a house. J. C. R.*); Frank Jewett Mather, Jr. (Lugt 1853a).

BIBLIOGRAPHY: Jacob Bean, "Chatsworth Drawings in America," *Master Drawings*, I, no. 1, 1963, p. 54.

Gift of Frank Jewett Mather, Jr., 47–14

JACOPO ROBUSTI, called TINTORETTO

Venice 1518 – Venice 1594

11 *Study of a Nude Male Figure*

Black chalk, on gray-brown paper; squared in black chalk. 10$\frac{15}{16}$ × 7$\frac{1}{4}$ inches (27.8 × 18.4 cm.).

Inscribed in pen and brown ink at lower right, *G Tintoretto*.

Study of a nude male figure in a pose used, as the Tietzes pointed out, for an angel that appears in Tintoretto's Resurrection of Christ, one of a series of ten canvases with scenes of the life of Christ painted for the Scuola di S. Rocco in Venice, between 1578 and 1581 (the Resurrection repr. H. Tietze, *Tintoretto*, London, 1948, pl. 202). A similar chalk study for another angel in the S. Rocco Resurrection was once, like the present drawing, in Joshua Reynolds's collection; its present whereabouts is unknown (repr. Tietze, *Venetian Drawings*, no. 1712, pl. CVIII,I).

PROVENANCE: Sir Joshua Reynolds (Lugt 2364); Frank Jewett Mather, Jr.

BIBLIOGRAPHY: Tietze, *Venetian Drawings*, no. 1758, said to be reproduced on pl. CVIII,I, but this plate in fact reproduces Tietze no. 1712.

EXHIBITIONS: Toronto, The Art Gallery of Toronto, Titian, Tintoretto, Paolo Veronese, 1960, no. 19.

Gift of Frank Jewett Mather, Jr., 46–83

ANDREA MELDOLLA, called SCHIAVONE

Zara 1522 – Venice 1563

12 *The Adoration of the Shepherds*

Brush and mauve wash, heightened with white, on gray-washed paper. 5¾ × 11¹¹⁄₁₆ inches (14.6 × 29.7 cm.). Surface abraded. Lined.

The rather drawn-out horizontal format of this drawing, as well as the mannered figure style closely dependent on Parmigianino, suggests a connection with the long panels depicting Biblical scenes painted by Schiavone for S. Maria del Carmelo in Venice. One of these panels, which now decorate the parapets of the choir lofts of the church, represents the Adoration of the Shepherds (the left half of the composition repr. B. Berenson, *Italian Pictures of the Renaissance. Venetian School*, II, London, 1957, pl. 1175). The figures in the panel are differently arranged—the Virgin is seated at center with the column behind her—but there is a striking stylistic affinity between this drawing and the panel.

PROVENANCE: Sir Peter Lely (Lugt 2092); Jonathan Richardson Senior (Lugt 2184); John Barnard (Lugt 1419); William Esdaile (Lugt 2617); Frank Jewett Mather, Jr. (Lugt 1853a).

Gift of Frank Jewett Mather, Jr., 48–1794

FEDERICO BAROCCI

Urbino 1526 – Urbino 1612

13 *Figure Studies*

Black and red chalk, heightened with white, a little brown wash, on blue paper. 10⅞ × 16¼ inches (27.7 × 41.3 cm.).

As Baird was the first to point out, these studies of a male torso, of a knee, of hands, and of a face with closed eyes are related to the figure of the dead Christ in Barocci's Entombment, painted in 1579–1582 for the high altar of the church of S. Croce in Senigállia (repr. Olsen, 1962, pl. 50). In his *catalogue raisonné* of Barocci's drawings, Olsen lists thirty-one sheets connectible with the Senigállia Deposition; seven of these include studies for the figure of Christ.

PROVENANCE: Sir Charles Greville (Lugt 549); Earl of Warwick (Lugt 2600); Warwick sale, London, Christie's, May 20, 1896, probably part of lot no. 14; Charles Fairfax Murray; sale, New York, Anderson Galleries, November 6–7, 1924, no. 214; Dan Fellows Platt (Lugt 750a).

BIBLIOGRAPHY: Thomas P. Baird, "Two Drawings Related to Baroccio's Entombment," *Record of The Art Museum. Princeton University*, IX, no. 1, 1950, pp. 11–16, fig. 2; Harald Olsen, *Federico Barocci. A Critical Study in Italian Cinquecento Painting* ("Figura," no. 6), Stockholm, 1955, p. 134; Harald Olsen, *Federico Barocci*, Copenhagen, 1962, p. 172.

Bequest of Dan Fellows Platt, 48–595

14 *Study of a Torso*

Black, white, and a little red chalk, on brown-washed paper. 16¹¹⁄₁₆ × 10⅜ inches (42.4 × 26.3 cm.).

This drawing and no. 15 below are studies for the figure of St. Sebastian, who stands at the left of the cross in the Crucifixion painted between 1590 and 1596 by Barocci for the cathedral of Genoa. The two drawings were first published with this identification by Agnes Mongan in 1932.

The monumental Crucifixion, signed and dated 1596, was commissioned by the Genoese Matteo Senarega, and still hangs in the Senarega Chapel in the cathedral (repr. Olsen, 1962, pl. 78). Further drawings by Barocci for the figure of St. Sebastian are preserved in the Uffizi and the Berlin Print Room.

PROVENANCE: Jonathan Richardson Senior (Lugt 2183); Charles Rogers (Lugt 624); Sir Charles Greville (Lugt 549); Earl of Warwick (Lugt 2600); Warwick sale, London, Christie's, May 20, 1896, part of lot no. 14; Charles Fairfax Murray; sale, New York, Anderson Galleries, November 6–7, 1924, no. 212; Dan Fellows Platt (Lugt 750a).

BIBLIOGRAPHY: Agnes Mongan, "Federigo Baroccio," *Old Master Drawings*, VII, no. 25, June 1932, pp. 5–6, pl. 12; Harald Olsen, *Federico Barocci. A Critical Study in Italian Cinquecento Painting* ("Figura," no. 6), Stockholm, 1955, p. 153; Harald Olsen, *Federico Barocci*, Copenhagen, 1962, p. 196.

EXHIBITIONS: Chicago, The Art Institute of Chicago, Drawings from the Collection of Dan Fellows Platt Loaned to the College Art Association, 1932, no. 15 or 16.

Bequest of Dan Fellows Platt, 48–598

15 Studies of Legs

Black, white, and a little red chalk, on brown-washed paper. $16\frac{7}{16} \times 10\frac{3}{4}$ inches (41.8×27.3 cm.).

See no. 14 above.

PROVENANCE: Jonathan Richardson Senior (Lugt 2183); Charles Rogers (Lugt 624); Sir Charles Greville (Lugt 549); Earl of Warwick (Lugt 2600); Warwick sale, London, Christie's, May 20, 1896, probably part of lot no. 14; Charles Fairfax Murray; sale, New York, Anderson Galleries, November 6–7, 1924, no. 213; Dan Fellows Platt (Lugt 750a).

BIBLIOGRAPHY: Agnes Mongan, "Federigo Baroccio," *Old Master Drawings*, VII, no. 25, June 1932, pp. 5–6, pl. 13; Harald Olsen, *Federico Barocci. A Critical Study in Italian Cinquecento Painting* ("Figura," no. 6), Stockholm, 1955, p. 153; Harald Olsen, *Federico Barocci*, Copenhagen, 1962, p. 196.

EXHIBITIONS: Chicago, The Art Institute of Chicago, Drawings from the Collection of Dan Fellows Platt Loaned to the College Art Association, 1932, no. 15 or 16.

Bequest of Dan Fellows Platt, 48–599

LUCA CAMBIASO
Moneglia 1527 – Madrid 1585

16 The Conversion of St. Paul

Pen and brown ink, brown wash, on brownish paper. $10\frac{15}{16} \times 16\frac{1}{16}$ inches (27.8×40.8 cm.). Numerous small losses. Lined.

Inscribed in pen and brown ink at lower right, *Canbiasio G.^{e}* [Genovese].

A characteristic exercise by Cambiaso in his "cubist" style. Suida Manning and Suida relate the drawing to other composition sketches for a projected Conversion of St. Paul, all datable after 1550.

This sheet bears an inscription in italic letters. Inscriptions in this hand, giving a draughtsman's name and place of birth, appear on numerous Italian drawings scattered in collections in Europe and America. The collector who so inscribed his drawings was very possibly Venetian, for the larger part of the sheets inscribed are Venetian in origin. His collecting activity seems to have come to an end before 1750, for no drawings bearing these inscriptions and datable in the second half of the century have so far appeared. This unidentified collector seems to have been an *amateur* of considerable taste and knowledge; the accuracy of his connoisseurship in Venetian draughtsmanship of the late seventeenth and early eighteenth centuries has won for him the convenient pseudonym of the "Reliable Venetian Hand" or "Reliable Italic Hand." Janos Scholz has suggested (*L'Arte*, XVIII, n.s., 1948–1951, p. 41) that the anonymous collector is identical with the celebrated Venetian *amateur* Antonio Maria Zanetti the Elder (1680–1757). Count Seilern, however, has pointed out several reasons that militate against this identification: the hand does not correspond with the several samples of handwriting identified as Zanetti's by F. Lugt (2992 f, g, and h); the inscriptions are not identical with those on Zanetti's chiaroscuro woodcuts; and, finally, inscriptions in the Reliable Hand are not found on any of the surviving drawings by Parmigianino that we know figured in Zanetti's own collection (A[ntoine] S[eilern], *Italian Paintings and Drawings at 56 Princes Gate . . .*, London, 1959, pp. 87–88). To these arguments may be added further evidence, supplied by a recently rediscovered manuscript inventory of the most important drawings belonging to a celebrated French collector, the Marquis de Lagoy (1764–1829). Like his near contemporary Vivant-Denon,

Lagoy acquired a number of fine drawings from Zanetti's heirs. Seventeen Italian drawings are described in the Lagoy inventory as coming from the Zanetti collection. Six of these seventeen sheets can today be identified in public collections abroad, and none of them bears an inscription in the hand of the anonymous and reliable collector. By title of example we cite in the British Museum an Adoration of the Magi by Parmigianino (1853-10-8-3), a study for the Borghese Entombment by Raphael (Philip Pouncey and J. A. Gere, *Italian Drawings . . . in the British Museum. Raphael and His Circle*, London, 1962, no. 12), and a design for a chapel by Perino del Vaga (Pouncey and Gere, *op. cit.*, no. 166). These three drawings are specifically given a Zanetti provenance in the Lagoy inventory, and they are not inscribed in the Reliable Venetian Hand.

PROVENANCE: "Reliable Venetian Hand" (Lugt 3005c–d); Robert Udny; Kaye Dowland (Lugt 691; inscribed on verso of old mount in pen and brown ink, *Kaye Dowland 1870 By Cambiaso of Genoa from the Udny Coll.ⁿ 1803 215E Very fine*); Miss Hill (Lugt 1313c); sale, London, Sotheby's, July 29, 1924, part of lot no. 79; Dan Fellows Platt (Lugt 2066b and 750a), purchased by Platt from Zilva.

BIBLIOGRAPHY: F. J. Mather, Jr., "The Platt Collection of Drawings," *Bulletin of the Department of Art and Archaeology, Princeton University*, June 1944, fig. 1; Bertina Suida Manning and William Suida, *Luca Cambiaso, la vita e le opere*, Milan, 1958, p. 199, pl. CXII, fig. 181.

EXHIBITIONS: Chicago, The Art Institute of Chicago, Drawings from the Collection of Dan Fellows Platt Loaned to the College Art Association, 1932, no. 23 or 24; Malmö, Utrecht, Birmingham, etc., American University Collections, organized by the College Art Association, 1956–1957.

Bequest of Dan Fellows Platt, 48–617

17   *The Return of Ulysses*

Pen and brown ink, brown wash, on brownish paper; squared in red chalk. 7¾×13⅝ inches (19.7×34.6 cm.). Losses at upper left. Lined.

When this drawing appeared at auction in New York in 1924, a correct and traditional attribution to Cambiaso was rejected in favor of one to Nicolas Poussin. The sheet is not only an excellent and typical example of Cambiaso's draughtsmanship, but Bertina Suida Manning and William Suida have pointed out that it is one of the artist's preparatory studies for the central panel on the ceiling of the Salone of the Palazzo della Meridiana in Genoa, an undertaking datable in the 1560s (repr. Suida Manning and Suida, fig. 162). Other composition studies for the Return of Ulysses, accompanied by his son Telemachus and under the protection of Minerva, are in the Teyler Museum in Haarlem and the Nationalmuseum in Stockholm.

PROVENANCE: Richard Cosway (Lugt 629); Charles Fairfax Murray; sale, New York, Anderson Galleries, November 7–8, 1924, no. 190 (as Nicolas Poussin); Professor Clifton R. Hall.

BIBLIOGRAPHY: Bertina Suida Manning and William Suida, *Luca Cambiaso, la vita e le opere*, Milan, 1958, p. 92, fig. 161 (mistakenly said to be from the Mather collection).

Laura P. Hall Memorial Collection, bequeathed by Professor Clifton R. Hall, 46–155

GIROLAMO MACCHIETTI
Florence 1535 – Florence 1592

18   *Seated Male Nude*

Red chalk, heightened with white, on yellow-brown washed paper; squared in black chalk. 8¼×6⁹⁄₁₆ inches (20.9×16.7 cm.). Repaired losses at upper and lower left, and at upper margin. Lined.

Inscribed in pen and brown ink at lower left, *Rosso*.

Formerly attributed to Rosso Fiorentino, this drawing was restored to Macchietti by Philip Pouncey, who pointed out its stylistic connection with the artist's figure studies for his representation of the healing baths at Pozzuoli, in the Studiolo of Francesco I de' Medici in the Palazzo Vecchio in Florence.

PROVENANCE: Dan Fellows Platt (Lugt 2066b and 750a), purchased by Platt from Parsons in 1925.

BIBLIOGRAPHY: Philip Pouncey, "Contribuito a Girolamo Macchietti," *Bollettino d'Arte*, XLVII, fourth series, 1962, pp. 237–240, fig. 3.

Bequest of Dan Fellows Platt, 48–579

BATTISTA NALDINI
Florence 1537 – Florence 1591

19   *Copy after Michelangelo's Guiliano de' Medici*

Black chalk, heightened with white, on brownish paper. 17³⁄₁₆×11½ inches (43.7

×29.2 cm.). Many brown spots on paper. Lined.

Inscribed in pen and brown ink at lower left corner, *Batista naldini da michelangiolo.*

Highly finished copy of Michelangelo's idealized marble figure of Giuliano de' Medici in the New Sacristy of S. Lorenzo in Florence. Naldini's draughtsmanship is here unusually restrained and "correct," but his personal manner, derived from his master Pontormo, may be observed in the wavering superimposed contours that delineate the hands and feet of the figure. The old inscription, attributing this handsome drawing to Naldini, is certainly correct. Naldini was one of the Florentine artists most closely involved in the commemoration of Michelangelo's genius after his death; he participated in the decoration of S. Lorenzo for the memorial service held July 1564, and he painted a Pietà that ornaments Michelangelo's tomb in S. Croce.

PROVENANCE: Lord Rowan (according to Goldstein sale catalogue); Dr. Max A. Goldstein, St. Louis; Goldstein sale, New York, American Art Galleries, March 2–5, 1920, no. 474; Dan Fellows Platt (Lugt 750a).

Bequest of Dan Fellows Platt, 48–762

20 *Copy after Michelangelo's Lorenzo de' Medici*

Black chalk, heightened with white, on brownish paper. 16$\frac{15}{16}$×11$\frac{1}{2}$ inches (43 × 29.2 cm.). Many brown spots on paper. Lined.

Inscribed in pen and brown ink in lower left corner, *Batista naldini da michelangiolo.*

An elaborately finished copy of Michelangelo's marble figure of Lorenzo de' Medici in the New Sacristy of S. Lorenzo in Florence. See no. 19 above.

PROVENANCE: Lord Rowan (according to Goldstein sale catalogue); Dr. Max A. Goldstein (Lugt 2824); Goldstein sale, New York, American Art Galleries, March 2–5, 1920, no. 473; Dan Fellows Platt (Lugt 750a).

Bequest of Dan Fellows Platt, 48–761

FEDERICO ZUCCARO
Sant'Angelo in Vado 1540/1541 – Ancona 1609

21 *Studies of the Head of a Bearded Man*

Black, red, and white chalk on blue paper. 7$\frac{1}{2}$×6$\frac{3}{8}$ inches (19 × 16.2 cm.). Lined.

This sheet was attributed by Professor Mather to Jacopo Bassano, and goes under this name in the Princeton inventory. Philip Pouncey was the first to point out that the neat use of *trois crayons* suggests instead the name of Federico Zuccaro, who did many such studies of heads.

PROVENANCE: John Rutson (Lugt 1517); Frank Jewett Mather, Jr. (Lugt 1853a).

EXHIBITIONS: Staten Island, Italian Drawings and Sculpture, 1958–1959, no. 13 (as Bassano).

Gift of Frank Jewett Mather, Jr., 47–122

JACOPO ZUCCHI

Florence 1541 – Florence or Rome 1589/1590

22 *The Age of Gold*

Pen and brown ink. $10\frac{15}{16} \times 8\frac{3}{8}$ inches (27.8 × 21.3 cm.). Repaired losses at lower right and left.

Inscribed in pen and brown ink at lower left, *Anironi [?] vandyck*

The source of the convincing attribution to Zucchi is unknown; the sheet itself bears only the obviously incorrect name of Van Dyck, but it figured in the Mather collection as the work of Zucchi. The scene represented is the mythological Age of Gold, set in a steep landscape that rises to a mountain crowned by the Tempio della Gloria, identified by an inscription. Bathers crowd the fore- and middle grounds, and at the left can be seen Pegasus, the Muses, and Apollo playing the fiddle. In overall composition and in many particulars the design is related to and may well be the study for Zucchi's picture in the Uffizi, representing the same subject (repr. H. Voss, *Die Malerei der Spätrenaissance in Rom und Florenz*, II, Berlin, 1920, p. 319). Zucchi's drawings are rare, but in style this sheet is reasonably compatible with a somewhat more elaborate design in Leipzig, given to the artist by Hermann Voss (repr. Voss, *op. cit.*, p. 323).

PROVENANCE: Victor Winthrop Newman (Lugt 2540); Frank Jewett Mather, Jr. (Lugt 1853a).

EXHIBITIONS: New York, Roerich Museum, 1930, no. 39.

Gift of Frank Jewett Mather, Jr., 47–151

JACOPO BERTOIA

Parma 1544 – Parma 1574

23 *Studies for a Seated Virgin and Child, and Other Figures*

VERSO:
Studies of Putti, a Cartouche, and Two Heads

Pen and brown ink, brown wash (recto). Pen and brown ink, brown wash; the three putti at upper right and right center are drawn in red chalk (verso). $16 \times 10\frac{11}{16}$ inches (40.7 × 27.2 cm.).

Inscribed in pen and brown ink at lower left corner, *Pelligrino da Modona*; on verso in pen and brown ink at lower left, *Polidoro da Caravaggio*; in pencil at lower margin, *Wilson 1937*; in pencil at upper margin, *Pellegro da Modena*.

Konrad Oberhuber has very recently proposed the convincing attribution to Bertoia for this double-faced sheet, formerly classed under the name of Polidoro da Caravaggio. The pen sketches on the recto may be compared with Bertoia's sheet of sketches in the British Museum for the Sala dei Sogni at Caprarola, where Bertoia worked for three successive summers in 1572, 1573, and 1574 (the London drawing repr. A. Ghidiglia Quintavalle, *Il Bertoja*, Milan, 1963, fig. 27). The beautiful red chalk and pen sketches of putti on the verso reveal the dominating influence of Parmigianino on Bertoia; the putto at the lower right with upraised arm is, as Popham points out, close to a putto holding a book in one of Bertoia's decorative friezes in the Oratorio del Gonfalone in Rome, where the artist worked before going to Caprarola (repr. Ghidiglia Quintavalle, *op. cit.*, pl. VIIIb).

27

PROVENANCE: Dan Fellows Platt (Lugt 750a), purchased by Platt from Wilson in 1937.

BIBLIOGRAPHY: Konrad Oberhuber, "Zu Jacopo Bertoia und Lelio Orsi," *Albertina Studien*, III, 1965, no. 1, pp. 26–27, fig. 5 (recto), fig. 6 (verso).

EXHIBITIONS: Staten Island, Italian Drawings and Sculpture, 1958–1959, no. 17 (as Michelangelo Merisi da Caravaggio).

Bequest of Dan Fellows Platt, 48–667

JACOPO PALMA, called PALMA GIOVANE

Venice 1544 – Venice 1628

24   *The Virgin and Child Appearing to Five Saints*

Pen and brown ink, brown wash, over black chalk; squared in red chalk. 11 × 6⅝ inches (27.9 × 16.8 cm.). Lined.

Verso: Figure sketches in pen and black ink, which are visible on recto.

The grouping of five saints below the Virgin, who appears surrounded by a glory of putti in the arched top of the vertical composition, is closely paralleled in an altarpiece by Palma Giovane in S. Zaccaria, Venice, datable in the opening years of the seventeenth century (repr. Adolfo Venturi, *Storia dell'arte italiana*, IX, Part 7, Milan, 1934, fig. 137). However, with the exception of the penitent Jerome, the cast of male saints in the S. Zaccaria altarpiece is different. A drawing certainly preparatory for this altarpiece is in the Morgan Library (repr. Tietze, no. 1051, pl. CLXXX,4). Though the design cannot be precisely related to a painted work, it is an eminently typical example of Palma Giovane's mature draughtsmanship.

PROVENANCE: Thomas Hudson (Lugt 2432); Sir Joshua Reynolds (Lugt 2364); Prince Wladimir Nikolaevitch Argoutinsky-Dolgoroukoff (Lugt 2602d); Argoutinsky-Dolgoroukoff sale, London, Sotheby's, July 4, 1923, no. 14; Frank Jewett Mather, Jr. (Lugt 1853a).

BIBLIOGRAPHY: Tietze, *Venetian Drawings*, no. 1243.

EXHIBITIONS: New York, Roerich Museum, 1930, no. 50.

Gift of Frank Jewett Mather, Jr., 44–268

25   *Back View of a Nude Male Figure*

Black chalk, heightened with white, on blue paper. 7⁷⁄₁₆ × 7¹³⁄₁₆ inches (18.9 × 19.8 cm.). Brown stains at upper right. Lined.

Inscribed in pen and brown ink at lower right, *Palma.*

The old inscription *Palma* gives us the correct lead; the drawing is an attractive example of Palma Giovane's chalk draughtsmanship.

PROVENANCE: Frank Jewett Mather, Jr. (Lugt 1853a).

Gift of Frank Jewett Mather, Jr., 51–35

ANDREA BOSCOLI
Florence 1550 – Florence 1606

26   *Frieze of Figures Bearing Offerings*

Pen and brown ink, brown wash, on light brown paper. 4⁷⁄₁₆ × 15⁵⁄₁₆ inches (11.3 × 38.9 cm.). Lined.

Inscribed in pen and black ink at lower right corner, *Polidori opus* and *16*.

The drawing is attributed in the Princeton inventory to Polidoro da Caravaggio, and, indeed, it is a copy of a section of Polidoro's now almost entirely effaced decoration on the façade of the Palazzo Milesi, via della Maschera d'Oro in Rome (engraved in E. Maccari's *Grafitti e chiaroscuri esistenti nell'esterno delle case*, Rome, 1876). Philip Pouncey recognized in this copy the highly personal, rather angular style of the Florentine Andrea Boscoli.

PROVENANCE: Pierre-Jean Mariette (Lugt 1852; the drawing cannot be identified in the catalogue of the 1775 Mariette sale); Count Mori[t]z von Fries (Lugt 2903); Dan Fellows Platt (Lugt 2066b and 750a), purchased by Platt from Parsons in 1929.

Bequest of Dan Fellows Platt, 48–666

ALESSANDRO CASOLANI
Siena 1552 – Siena 1606

27 *Nude Youth Resting Against the Leg of Another Figure*

Black chalk on brownish paper. $5\frac{3}{16} \times 6\frac{7}{16}$ inches (13.2 × 16.4 cm.).

Inscribed in pen and brown ink at lower right, *Cassolani*.

A characteristic example of Casolani's rather weak but certainly attractive style as a figure draughtsman.

PROVENANCE: Dan Fellows Platt (2066b and 750a), purchased by Platt from De Clementi in 1924.

Bequest of Dan Fellows Platt, 48–677

ANNIBALE CARRACCI
Bologna 1560 – Rome 1609

28 *Portrait of a Young Man*

Red chalk. $16\frac{1}{8} \times 10\frac{7}{8}$ inches (41 × 27.7 cm.).

A striking and only recently rediscovered example of the drawn portraiture that was something of a specialty in the circle of the Carracci. Here the identity of the model is unknown. The broad handling of the red chalk is close to that of the few portrait drawings that may be attributed with certainty to Annibale himself, but the attribution seems justified above all by the force of the portrait image.

PROVENANCE: Seiferheld and Co., New York; Miss Margaret Mower, New York.

Gift of Miss Margaret Mower for the Elsa Durand Mower Collection, 62.51

DOMENICO TINTORETTO
Venice 1560 – Venice 1635

29 *The Virgin Interceding before Christ for Plague-Stricken Venice*

Brush, red, cream, and brown oil paint on brownish paper. $15\frac{13}{16} \times 7\frac{11}{16}$ inches (40.2 × 19.5 cm.). Lined.

Rosanna Tozzi connected this oil sketch with Domenico Tintoretto's Venetian plague banner of 1631 in S. Francesco della Vigna, representing the allegorical figure of Venice imploring the mediation of the Virgin for the cessation of the plague. The picture corresponds in all essentials to Domenico's oil sketch; the banderole that divides the vertical composition at its center bears in the finished work the text of a plea addressed by the city of Venice to the Virgin as Mediatrix. Domenico's figure style, even in this very late work, shows a close dependence on that of his father Jacopo, but the technique of the drawing, where oil paint is broadly brushed on paper to achieve the effect of a small painted *bozzetto*, is very characteristic of Domenico.

PROVENANCE: Frank Jewett Mather, Jr. (Lugt 1853a).

BIBLIOGRAPHY: Rosanna Tozzi, "Disegni di Domenico Tintoretto," *Bollettino d'Arte*, XXXI, 1937–1938, p. 22, repr. p. 21, fig. 3; Tietze, *Venetian Drawings*, 1944, no. 1554, pl. CXX,4.

EXHIBITIONS: New York, Roerich Museum, 1930, no. 51a; Toronto, The Art Gallery of Toronto, Titian, Tintoretto, Paolo Veronese, 1960, no. 31.

Gift of Frank Jewett Mather, Jr., 48–1919

30   *The Adoration of the Shepherds*

Brush, cream, black, brown, and a little red oil paint on gray-green paper. $15\frac{1}{16} \times 7\frac{13}{16}$ inches (38.3 × 19.8 cm.).

Stylistically similar to the previous drawing, datable 1631, this excellent example of Domenico's brush draughtsmanship must be a late work. It cannot be related to a surviving picture.

PROVENANCE: Unidentified collector's mark at upper left; another unidentified mark on verso; Frank Jewett Mather, Jr. (Lugt 1853a).

BIBLIOGRAPHY: Tietze, *Venetian Drawings*, no. 1555.

EXHIBITIONS: New York, Roerich Museum, 1930, no. 51; Toronto, The Art Gallery of Toronto, Titian, Tintoretto, Paolo Veronese, 1960, no. 32.

Gift of Frank Jewett Mather, Jr., 48–1920

FERRAÙ FENZONI
Faenza 1562 – Faenza 1645

31   *The Massacre of the Innocents*

Pen and brown ink on light brown paper. $7\frac{5}{8} \times 10\frac{3}{16}$ inches (19.4 × 25.9 cm.). Unidentified paraph in pen and brown ink at lower left corner. Lined.

This drawing had been classified as anonymous Venetian, sixteenth century, until Philip Pouncey, in 1958, recognized it as a characteristic example of the draughtsmanship of Ferraù Fenzoni. The repetitive round facial types and the agitated pen work are typical of the artist.

PROVENANCE: Charles Fairfax Murray; sale, New York, Anderson Galleries, November 6–7, 1924, no. 256 (attributed to Tintoretto); Frank Jewett Mather, Jr.

Gift of Frank Jewett Mather, Jr., 47–76

REMIGIO CANTAGALLINA
Florence 1582 – Florence, after 1630

32   *View of a Village Square and Church*

Pen and brown ink, brown wash, over black chalk. $9\frac{11}{16} \times 15\frac{3}{8}$ inches (24.6 × 39 cm.).

Inscribed in pen and brown ink at lower left, *6 di luglio 1633*.

An exceptionally attractive example of Cantagallina's specialty, Tuscan landscape views.

PROVENANCE: Mathias Komor (Lugt 1882a); purchased by The Art Museum from Komor in 1956.

Laura P. Hall Memorial Fund, 56-32

MARCANTONIO BASSETTI
Verona 1588 – Verona 1630

33 *The Martyrdom of the Ten Thousand*

Pen and brown ink, brown wash, heightened with white, on brown-washed paper. $7\frac{13}{16} \times 5\frac{3}{4}$ inches (19.8 × 14.6 cm.). Lined.

Inscribed in pen and brown ink on old mount at lower left, *Basseti Veronesi*.

The old inscription on the mount of the drawing supplies the certainly correct attribution to Bassetti, and this unpublished example joins the drawn *oeuvre* of this little-known Veronese master. Following the lead of Roberto Longhi and A. E. Popham, Sir Anthony Blunt has well described the very personal style of Bassetti, who is richly represented at Windsor: "His drawings are executed in the late sixteenth-century Venetian method of almost grisaille oils on paper, but they are characterized by a type of closed composition with the figures crowded into the front of the space, and by a method of modelling the form in little lumps or knots, emphasized by the strong highlights added in pure white pigment" (Anthony Blunt and Edward Croft-Murray, *Venetian Drawings of the XVII and XVIII Centuries . . . at Windsor Castle*, London, 1957, p. 25).

PROVENANCE: Frothingham (according to pencil inscription on mount); Frank Jewett Mather, Jr.

Gift of Frank Jewett Mather, Jr., 47–124

GIOVANNI FRANCESCO BARBIERI, called GUERCINO
Cento 1591 – Bologna 1666

34 *Madonna and Child with St. Anthony of Padua*

Pen and two shades of brown ink, brown wash. $9\frac{7}{16} \times 6\frac{9}{16}$ inches (24 × 16.6 cm.).

A fine early drawing, dated by Mahon about 1616–1618; it cannot be connected with a surviving picture. Various *pentimenti*, especially in the head and the arms of the kneeling Anthony, were made by Guercino in a brown ink paler than that used for the design as a whole.

PROVENANCE: Dan Fellows Platt (Lugt 750a), purchased by Platt from Richeton in London in 1922.

BIBLIOGRAPHY: Lynes, *Platt Guercino Drawings*, p. 91, no. 66.

Bequest of Dan Fellows Platt, 48–1267

35 *A Couple Conversing*

Pen and brown ink. $7\frac{1}{2} \times 10\frac{1}{4}$ inches (19.1 × 26 cm.).

Mrs. Lynes lists this drawing as a representation of the Denial of St. Peter, and it is indeed possible that the two figures are studied for such a composition. Mahon dates the drawing about 1624. The border of the old mount, ornamented with a pattern of parallel pen lines, is the sign of an excellent provenance—the collection of Guercino's nephews Benedetto and Cesare Gennari.

PROVENANCE: Gennari (Lugt 2858c); Dan Fellows Platt (Lugt 750a).

BIBLIOGRAPHY: Lynes, *Platt Guercino Drawings*, p. 103, no. 103.

Bequest of Dan Fellows Platt, 48–727

36   *The Arrest of Christ*

Pen and brown ink, brown wash, on brownish paper. $7\frac{13}{16} \times 11\frac{7}{8}$ inches (19.8 ×30.2 cm.). Paper considerably foxed. Lined.

A superb example of Guercino's early style—"d'une touche énergique et facile," as the 1780 Nogaret sale catalogue aptly puts it. Mahon dates the drawing in the late 1620s.

PROVENANCE: Nogaret; Nogaret sale, Paris, June 2, 1780, no. 68; Chariot; Chariot sale, Paris, January 28, 1788, no. 87; Daudet (Inscribed in pen and brown ink on verso of old mount, *Daudet. Ce 18. février 1788. Ce dessin provient de la vente de M. Chariot huissier Commissaire priseur qui s'est faite vers la fin de janvier de la dite année et qui m'a couté 251.1.⁸*.); Dan Fellows Platt (Lugt 750a), purchased by Platt from Parsons in 1923.

BIBLIOGRAPHY: Lynes, *Platt Guercino Drawings*, p. 95, no. 76.

Bequest of Dan Fellows Platt, 48–744

37   *Kneeling Penitent Saint*

Pen and brown ink, brown wash, on brownish paper. $10\frac{1}{4} \times 7\frac{3}{4}$ inches (26.1 × 19.6 cm.). Lined.

Inscribed in pen and brown ink at lower left corner, *Guercino*.

Mahon places this drawing, in which transparent wash is used with great freedom, about 1630.

PROVENANCE: Sir Joshua Reynolds (Lugt 2364); William Bateson (Lugt 2604a); Dan Fellows Platt (Lugt 2066b and 750a), purchased by Platt from Parsons in 1929.

BIBLIOGRAPHY: Lynes, *Platt Guercino Drawings*, p. 100, no. 93.

Bequest of Dan Fellows Platt, 49–44

38   *Half Figure of St. Joseph Holding a Staff*

Pen and brown ink, brown wash. $6\frac{1}{4} \times 8\frac{1}{8}$ inches (15.9 ×20.6 cm.).

Mahon suggests that this sheet could be dated in the 1630s.

PROVENANCE: Edward Bouverie (Lugt 325); Dan Fellows Platt (Lugt 750a), purchased by Platt from Parsons in 1922.

BIBLIOGRAPHY: Lynes, *Platt Guercino Drawings*, p. 95, no. 78.

Bequest of Dan Fellows Platt, 49–40

39   *The Visitation*

Pen and brown ink, pale gray-brown wash. $7\frac{13}{16} \times 8\frac{3}{4}$ inches (19.8 ×22.2 cm.). Vertical crease at left.

Verso: Pen and brown ink study of Elizabeth embracing the Virgin.

Denis Mahon has identified this drawing as a preparatory study for a Visitation painted by Guercino in 1632 for the Duomo at Reggio Emilia and now in the Rouen Museum (repr. Nefta Grimaldi, *Il Guercino*, Bologna, n.d., pl. 98, where the caption wrongly places the picture in the Museo Nazionale, Rome). Guercino supplied a Martyrdom of St. John and St. Paul, now in the Musée des Augustins in Toulouse, for the Reggio Duomo at the same time; the two pictures are mentioned by Malvasia, and full payment recorded in Guercino's account book in June 7, 1632 (Malvasia, *Felsina Pittrice*, Bolognese edition of 1841, II, pp. 262 and 310). Two composition studies for the Visitation in the Morgan Library (no. I, 101F, and 1956–21) are closer to the picture, in which both Mary and Elizabeth are standing, than to the Princeton drawing where Elizabeth tenderly assists the Virgin Mary in dismounting. On the verso of the sheet there is a sketch of Elizabeth kissing the Virgin, another motif not utilized in the painting.

PROVENANCE: Dan Fellows Platt (Lugt 750a), purchased by Platt from Parsons in 1920.

BIBLIOGRAPHY: Lynes, *Platt Guercino Drawings*, p. 93, no. 71.

Bequest of Dan Fellows Platt, 48–745

40 *The Martyrdom of St. Bartholomew*

Pen and brown ink, brown wash. 8 × 10 inches (20.3 × 25.4 cm.).

First payment for a Martyrdom of St. Bartholomew, commissioned for the church of S. Martino in Siena, is mentioned in Guercino's account book under September 1, 1636; a bonus of 200 *ducatoni* and fourteen arm's-lengths of *peluzzo di Siena*, in addition to the agreed price of 600 *ducatoni*, is recorded on April 8, 1637 (Malvasia, *Felsina Pittrice*, Bolognese edition of 1841, II, pp. 263, 315, 316). The picture, now much damaged, still hangs in S. Martino. A contemporary copy, now in the church of S. Barnaba at Marino near Rome, was painted for Cardinal Colonna, Archbishop of Bologna, by Giacinto Campana and retouched according to Malvasia by Guercino himself. It gives a clearer idea of the composition than the ruined original. Denis Mahon has pointed out the connection of the dramatic Princeton drawing with the Siena picture, and he has related drawings at the Morgan Library (no. I, 101E) and the Art Institute of Chicago (no. 60.832) to the same altarpiece. Each of the drawings records strikingly different solutions for this commission, and all differ from the more classic solution adopted in the painting.

PROVENANCE: William Bateson (Lugt 2604a); Dan Fellows Platt (Lugt 2066b and 750a), purchased by Platt from Parsons in 1929.

BIBLIOGRAPHY: Lynes, *Platt Guercino Drawings*, p. 96, no. 79.

Bequest of Dan Fellows Platt, 48–734

41 *Cephalus Mourning the Dead Procris*

Pen and brown ink, brown wash. 8 1/8 × 11 inches (20.6 × 27.9 cm.). Lower margin torn irregularly. Lined.

Inscribed in pen and dark brown ink at lower left corner, *Guercino*.

This composition study is closely related to other sheets representing the same subject. Dan Fellows Platt owned three studies for a composition representing Cephalus and Procris: the present fine example; an unconvincing pale black chalk drawing (Princeton 49–17) varying in many details from the sheet here exhibited; and a pen and wash version with Cephalus in an upright position, with his right knee on a rock. The latter was sold from the Platt collection in 1949, and its present whereabouts is unknown.

Mariette possessed a pen study for Cephalus and Procris, close to the sheet here exhibited, but in which Cephalus rests his head on his hand. Mariette's drawing was engraved in reverse by Vincenzo Vangelisti and published in the Boydells' *Seventy-Three Prints . . . in the Collection of His Majesty, etc.* (II, London, n.d., pl. 68) with the caption: *Disegno del Guercino già nella raccolta di Crozat oggi in quella di M. Mariette. Il quadro poco variato stà nella Galleria di Dresda*. In the Dresden picture, commissioned in 1644 by Marchese Cornelio Bentivoglio for Anne d'Autriche, Queen of France, and unfortunately destroyed in World War II, Cephalus is seated at the left of the composition and looks upward to the left, not to the right as in the present study (the Dresden picture repr. H. Ebert, *Kriegsverluste der Dresdner Gemäldegalerie*, Dresden, 1963, p. 33, no. 361). Mahon points out that though at first sight the drawing appears relatively early in style, the connections with the picture formerly at Dresden are such that one has to presume it is a preparatory study. Thus, it must date from 1644.

An old copy of the present drawing is at Dijon (no. 768, Gernsheim photo 4355); this once belonged to Baron Vivant-Denon, who reproduced it in his *Monuments des arts du dessin* (III, pl. 208), while the weak Princeton black chalk version mentioned above is a copy of Mariette's drawing.

PROVENANCE: Dan Fellows Platt (Lugt 750a), purchased by Platt from Parsons in 1922.

BIBLIOGRAPHY: Lynes, *Platt Guercino Drawings*, p. 87, no. 54.

Bequest of Dan Fellows Platt, 48–733

42 *Head of a Bearded Man Looking Down*

Pen and brown ink. $4\frac{13}{16} \times 6\frac{5}{16}$ inches (12.2 × 16 cm.).

Verso: End of a letter signed by Guercino and dated Cento, August 30, 1631.

This sheet was originally used for the draft of a letter signed by Guercino and dated 1631; it then was cut up and used for drawing—a good deal later, it would seem in this case. The following pen study of a head is stylistically very close to the present example, and should be of approximately the same date; yet no. 43 is drawn on the draft of a letter dated ten years later, in 1641.

PROVENANCE: Dan Fellows Platt (Lugt 2066b and 750a), purchased by Platt from Parsons in 1920.

BIBLIOGRAPHY: Lynes, *Platt Guercino Drawings*, p. 125, no. 177.

Bequest of Dan Fellows Platt, 48–712

43 Profile of a Man Facing Right

Pen and brown ink. 6 7/8 × 5 7/16 inches (17.4 × 13.8 cm.).

Inscribed in pen and brown ink in lower right corner, *34 P. Dol.*

Verso: The end of a letter in Guercino's hand, dated 1641.

The date, 1641, on the fragment draft of a letter that Guercino turned over and used for this sketch, gives us a useful *terminus post quem* for the date of this drawing. Denis Mahon suggests that the inscription *34 P. Dol.* at the lower right corner may be an inventory number used in the Gennari collection, a prime source of Guercino drawings. Another Guercino head at Princeton (48–704) bears the inscription *35 P. Do..* These small sheets do not have the usual Gennari border (see Lugt 2858c), but the present example, according to Platt's inscription, came from the collection of the Earl of Gainsborough, who obtained his Guercino drawings from the Gennari collection.

PROVENANCE: [Earl of] Gainsborough (according to note by Platt on verso); Dan Fellows Platt (Lugt 750a), purchased by Platt from Parsons in 1924.

Bequest of Dan Fellows Platt, 48–713

44 Head of a Pope

Pen and brown ink. 4 7/8 × 5 1/4 inches (12.4 × 13.3 cm.).

An incisive head where the representation verges on caricature, a vein in which Guercino excelled.

PROVENANCE: Dan Fellows Platt (Lugt 750a), purchased by Platt from Parsons in 1920.

BIBLIOGRAPHY: Lynes, *Platt Guercino Drawings*, p. 109, no. 118.

Bequest of Dan Fellows Platt, 48–716

45 Page from a Sketchbook—Caricature of a Boy Wearing a Broad-Brimmed Hat

Pen and brown ink, brown wash. 6 7/16 × 4 3/4 inches (16.3 × 12.1 cm.). Loss above center. Lined.

This exceptionally spirited and touching drawing and the following examples (nos. 46, 47) form part of a fascinating series of caricatures by Guercino, acquired by Dan Fellows Platt in London in 1928. The drawings are mounted in an album with pages measuring 288 × 210 mm., ornamented with an eighteenth-century frontispiece in the form of an architectural tablet inscribed: *Diverse caricature disegnate a penna e aquarrella di Gio: Francesco Barbieri detto il Guercino da Cento.* The tablet is surmounted by a drawn portrait of the artist. A hand-lettered preface gives a brief biography of Guercino, and singles out his talent as a caricaturist, *Dono poi suo particolare fu ancora il fare certi ritratti, che Noi Pitori chiamiamo Carricature, nel qual genere di cose egli fu uno di quei pochi dotati di quella vivacità, e mente, che a ciò fare abbisogna, e da locare trà più Eccellenti, come furono, parlando, de' nostri, Anibale principalmente, e Agostino Caracci, e quindi Leonello Spada, e il Tiarini.* (One of his particular gifts was making certain portraits that our painters call caricatures, a kind of thing in which he was one of those few gifted with the vivacity and in-

35

telligence that this sort of thing requires; and he stands amongst the very best, such as, speaking of our painters, Annibale especially and Agostino Carracci, and then Lionello Spada and Tiarini.)

The pages of the volume are numbered from one to twenty-eight in red chalk, but as Platt pointed out in a pencil note on the flyleaf, five leaves had been removed from the album before the red numbers were inscribed. When Platt acquired the volume in 1928 from P. W. Holoway, nine leaves had already been removed by the Savile Gallery through whose hands the album had passed. A year later Platt was fortunate enough to acquire these nine leaves, and restore them to the original series. At a later date Platt added six leaves extraneous to the album, and attached to these leaves drawings attributed to Guercino that he had acquired in the early 1920s. He further attached an extraneous drawing to a page of the original album, from which a caricature study by Guercino had been removed (the gall-nut ink impression of this drawing, a study of four heads in profile, remains on the page). All of the drawings originally in the album can be given to Guercino himself, while the seven extraneous leaves added by Platt appear to be eighteenth-century pastiches of Guercino.

Only two of the original pages bear inscriptions, and these are not contemporary with the drawings. Below the fourteenth sheet in the album, A Head of a Man in Profile to the Left, there is an old inscription, *Caricatura di Anibale Caracci, di mano del Guercino da Cento*. The drawing, however, in no way resembles and can hardly be a caricature of Annibale. That this inscription dates from the eighteenth century and not from the seven-

teenth is clear from a comment in the same handwriting on a later page bearing a savage caricature of two men with faces resembling animal snouts. The inscription beneath reads *Questa caricatura somiglia moltissimo al Barone Stosch* (this caricature very much resembles Baron Stosch). Philip von Stosch (1691–1757) arrived in 1715 in Rome where he was employed by Cardinal Alessandro Albani.

In the present exhibition the album is shown open at the page bearing no. 45. The two framed drawings (nos. 46, 47) are chosen from the pages cut out of the book before 1928 and later loosely reattached by Platt. Their temporary removal from the album in no way affects what remains of the original binding.

PROVENANCE: Sir Joshua Reynolds (according to inscription on title page); the later history of the album is somewhat difficult to reconstruct from the several inscriptions on the title page: in pen and brown ink, *From the Collection of Sir Joshua Reynolds Given to Mr. Price Nov. 28, 1881. John Palmer. Lieut Colonel.*; in pen and black ink in another hand, *Mr. E. Price to Mrs. Clara J. Pearce*; in pencil in yet another hand, *My mother R-G: W E Price married Anne Palmer, sister of my mother and gr-niece of Sir Joshua, she had no issue, hence the gift to my mother*; Savile Gallery, London; Dan Fellows Platt (Lugt 2066b), purchased by Platt from Holoway in 1928.

BIBLIOGRAPHY: *International Studio*, XCI, November 1928, p. 54, repr.; Lynes, *Platt Guercino Drawings*, p. 79, no. 25; Max Kozloff, "The Caricatures of Giambattista Tiepolo," *Marsyas*, X, 1960–1961, fig. 10, opp. p. 17.

Bequest of Dan Fellows Platt, 48-1294

46 *Caricature of a Woman with Deformed Lips*

Pen and brown ink, brown wash. 6⁹⁄₁₆ × 6½ inches (16.7 × 16.5 cm.).

Verso: Fragment of a landscape in pen and brown ink.

See no. 45 above.

PROVENANCE: See no. 45 above.

BIBLIOGRAPHY: Lynes, *Platt Guercino Drawings*, p. 82, no. 34.

Bequest of Dan Fellows Platt, 48–1302

47 *Caricature of a Man in a Cap with Hands Crossed on His Chest*

Pen and brown ink, brown wash. 10³⁄₁₆ × 6⅜ inches (25.9 × 16.2 cm.). Lined.

See no. 45 above.

PROVENANCE: See no. 45 above.

BIBLIOGRAPHY: Lynes, *Platt Guercino Drawings*, p. 83, no. 41.

Bequest of Dan Fellows Platt, 48–1309

48 *Veronica's Veil Imprinted with the Face of Christ*

Pen and brown ink. Diameter 7¹⁄₁₆ inches (17.9 cm.). Scattered losses due to acid ink.

This emblematic drawing, in which two putti hold up Veronica's veil, above the head of John the Baptist resting in a platter, is very probably the sheet belonging to Prince Abbondio Rezzonico that was engraved in reverse by James Nevay in G. B. Piranesi's *Raccolta di alcuni disegni del . . . Guercino*, published in 1767. The pen work is somewhat dry and schematic,

and the design no doubt dates from fairly late in Guercino's career. As Denis Mahon has pointed out, the real interest of the drawing is that stylistically and technically it can be compared so instructively with a late eighteenth-century copy at Princeton (no. 49 below) that stands as a token of a vast group of copies after Guercino drawings or, rather, after engravings reproducing them. Guercino's characteristic use in the present drawing of an acid ink that has eaten into the paper should be noted in contrast to the thick, pasty ink, flaked off in certain passages, that is so noticeable in the following copy and in hundreds of other deceptive late eighteenth-century copies after Guercino.

PROVENANCE: Prince Abbondio Rezzonico; William Young Ottley (on an Ottley mount with his attribution, *Il Guercino da Cento, Pitt.*); William Esdaile (Lugt 2617, inscribed on verso, *1814 WE P8 N600*); Dan Fellows Platt (Lugt 2066b and 750a), purchased by Platt from Parsons in 1923.

BIBLIOGRAPHY: Giovanni Battista Piranesi, *Raccolta di alcuni disegni del Barbieri da Cento detto il Guercino . . .*, Rome [1767], no. 4, engraved in reverse by James Nevay; Lynes, *Platt Guercino Drawings*, p. 103, no. 101.

Bequest of Dan Fellows Platt, 49–30

GUERCINO, Copy after

49 *Veronica's Veil*

Pen and brown ink, thick brown wash. 7¹³⁄₁₆ × 6¹³⁄₁₆ inches (19.8 × 17.3 cm.). Paper considerably foxed. Lined.

Inscribed in pen and brown ink on the old mount, *Originale di Gio: Francesco Barbieri, detto Guercino.*

Free copy in reverse of the preceding drawing, no. 48. The reversal of the composition would seem to prove that this unintelligent and unattractive copy was made not directly from Guercino's original drawing but from the reversed reproduction of it in Piranesi's 1767 publication. This drawing, as Mahon suggests, is a typical example of a mass of copies or pastiches of Guercino's drawings, usually executed in thick pasty ink, no doubt with deceptive intention. That these copies were not made before the second half of the eighteenth century is clear, since the present example is a copy of an engraving published in 1767. The Princeton collection is fortunate in possessing this instructive pair of drawings, Guercino's original and a deceptive copy thereof.

PROVENANCE: Dan Fellows Platt (Lugt 2066b and 750a), purchased by Platt from Parsons in 1928.

BIBLIOGRAPHY: Lynes, *Platt Guercino Drawings*, p. 102, no. 100 (listed as an original drawing by Guercino).

Bequest of Dan Fellows Platt, 49–29

PIETRO BERRETTINI, called PIETRO DA CORTONA
Cortona 1596 – Rome 1669

50 *Study for the Age of Iron*

Pen and brown ink, over red chalk, on light brown paper. 12 1/4 × 10 3/16 inches (31.1 × 25.9 cm.). Lined.

The drawing is traditionally attributed to Pietro da Cortona, and Coffin has pointed out that it is a study for one of the four frescoes in the Camera della Stufa of the Palazzo Pitti in Florence. Cortona, who had arrived in Florence from Rome in July 1637, received this commission from Ferdinando II de' Medici. By September of the same year two of the frescoes, the Age of Silver and the Age of Gold, were finished, and Cortona departed for Venice. At the end of the year he rushed back to Rome to continue work on the ceiling frescoes in the Salone of the Palazzo Barberini; only in the summer of 1640 was he able to return to Florence and finish the two further compositions in the Camera della Stufa, the Age of Iron and the Age of Bronze. The Princeton drawing for the Age of Iron is the only surviving study for this fresco, but a good many preparatory drawings for the three other compositions have survived. With the Princeton sheet these drawings form a stylistically consistent group, and they all no doubt date from the first Florentine stay in 1637, when the decorative cycle was planned. The Four Ages of Man as recounted by Ovid in the *Metamorphoses* are the subject of the frescoes. Ovid's sequence, which runs from the delights of the Age of Gold to the horrors of the Age of Iron, is pessimistic, and Vitzthum has suggested that Cortona's iconographical program reverses this order and represents a happy progress from the Age of Iron to the Age of Gold. The latter fresco contains specific references to a contemporary event, the marriage of Ferdinando II de' Medici to Vittoria della Rovere. A significant variation between the Princeton study and the finished fresco representing the Age of Iron gives evidence to support this thesis. In the drawing a soldier at the left attacks a Christian priest, identified as such by the crucifix indicated at the left margin; in the fresco the statue of a goddess under a portico identifies the building as a pagan temple. If the Age of Iron is the first composition in the allegorical cycle, then the temple must for the sake of chronological accuracy be pagan. The presence of a Christian priest in the Princeton drawing is an anachronism corrected in the fresco itself.

PROVENANCE: William Young Ottley (according to inscription on verso); Dan Fellows Platt (Lugt 2066b and 750a), purchased by Platt from Holoway in 1923.

BIBLIOGRAPHY: David R. Coffin, "A Drawing by Pietro da Cortona for his Fresco of the Age of Iron," *Record of The Art Museum. Princeton University*, XIII, no. 2, 1954, pp. 33–37, fig. 1; Malcolm Campbell and Myron Laskin, Jr., "A New Drawing for Pietro da Cortona's 'Age of Bronze,'" *Burlington Magazine*, CIII, 1961, pp. 423–427, fig. 23; Walter Vitzthum and Malcolm Campbell, correspondence in *Burlington Magazine*, CIV, 1962, pp. 120–125; Malcolm Campbell, *Gabinetto Disegni e Stampe degli Uffizi. XXI. Mostra di disegni di Pietro Berretini da Cortona per gli affreschi di Palazzo Pitti*, Florence, 1965, p. 17, note, p. 24.

Bequest of Dan Fellows Platt, 48–772

GIOVANNI BENEDETTO CASTIGLIONE

Genoa about 1600 – Mantua 1665

51 *Joseph Interpreting Dreams*

Pen and brown ink on light brown paper. Horizontal black chalk line at lower right. 8 5/16 × 11 1/2 inches (21.2 × 29.3 cm.).

Repaired losses at center and upper right.

Verso: Pen studies of two figures, one lifting a heavy object.

This drawing was acquired by Dan Fellows Platt from Parsons in London as part of an important series of sketches by Salvator Rosa (see nos. 56, 58–64), and it retained this attribution in the Princeton inventory. The style of the pen work is not, however, that of Rosa; the energetic parallel hatching and the facial types clearly point to Giovanni Benedetto Castiglione, who is certainly the draughtsman here. The sheet may be compared with free pen sketches by Castiglione at Windsor Castle, where the better part of the artist's drawn *oeuvre* is conserved (see Anthony Blunt, *The Drawings of G. B. Castiglione and Stefano della Bella . . . at Windsor Castle*, London, 1954, particularly pls. 17, 18, 28, and 29). The pen studies on the verso of the sheet, representing a figure lifting an object, may well be connected with the artist's representation of the myth of Deucalion and Pyrrha. The picture is in Berlin (Inv. no. 2078), and related drawings are at Windsor (Blunt, *op. cit.*, nos. 150 and 244).

PROVENANCE: Dan Fellows Platt (Lugt 2066b and 750a), purchased by Platt from Parsons in 1929.

Bequest of Dan Fellows Platt, 48–811

FRANCESCO MONTELATICI, called CECCO BRAVO

Florence, about 1600 – Innsbruck 1661

52 *Reclining Youth*

Red chalk on brownish paper. 10 13/16 × 14 1/2 inches (27.5 × 36.9 cm.). Repaired losses at upper center and lower margin. Numerous oil stains.

Inscribed in two hands (?) in red chalk at lower right corner, *Cecca Salviati*.

This typically Florentine chalk study of a youthful model came to Princeton with an attribution to Francesco Salviati. The erroneous identification is no doubt based on the inscription at lower right: to the word *Cecca* (more correctly *Cecco*), Francesco Montelatici's nickname, has been added, possibly in another hand, the name *Salviati*. Montelatici and Salviati had the same nickname, Cecco or Cecchino, short for Francesco. The present drawing, however, has nothing to do with Salviati, and is instead a typical example of Cecco Bravo's figure style. The draughtsmanship harks back to Andrea del Sarto and Pontormo, but contour and form tend to be dissolved in flickering light in a fashion typical of this later Tuscan.

PROVENANCE: Frank Jewett Mather, Jr. (Lugt 1853a).

EXHIBITIONS: New York, Roerich Museum, 1930, no. 32 (as Francesco Salviati).

Gift of Frank Jewett Mather, Jr., 47–141

PIER FRANCESCO MOLA

Coldrerio 1612 – Rome 1666

53   *The Flight into Egypt*

Pen and brown ink, brown wash, over red wash. 7¼ × 10 1/16 inches (18.5 × 25.6 cm.). All four corners trimmed.

Inscribed in pen and brown ink at lower right corner, *40*; on verso, *gio. francesco*

Barbieri dit le Guerchin de Cento. 1590+ 1666.

The French inscription on the verso suggests an attribution to Guercino; Professor Mather gave it to Sébastien Bourdon, and it has figured under this name in the Princeton inventory. The style of the sheet, however, proclaims it to be the work of Pier Francesco Mola. The composition is a lyrical reinterpretation of Annibale Carracci's Landscape with the Flight into Egypt, one of the lunettes painted for the chapel of the Palazzo Aldobrandini and now in the Galleria Doria-Pamphilj in Rome (repr. H. Voss, *Die Malerei des Barock in Rom*, Berlin, 1924, p. 177). Mola has even taken over from Annibale's landscape a Bolognese boatman, who navigates a small craft in the left middle ground. In style the present drawing may be compared with a Rest on the Flight in the Cabinet des Dessins of the Louvre, traditionally and correctly attributed to Mola, which must date from the Bolognese-inspired period of Mola's career (Inv. 8414; repr. *Master Drawings*, II, no. 3, 1964, pl. 24a).

PROVENANCE: Frank Jewett Mather, Jr. (Lugt 1853a).

EXHIBITIONS: New York, Roerich Museum, 1930, no. 91 (as Bourdon).

Gift of Frank Jewett Mather, Jr., 52–195

54   *Joseph Interpreting Dreams*

Pen and brown ink, brown wash, over red and black chalk. 7 1/16 × 6¾ inches (17.9 × 17.2 cm.). Lined.

A somewhat stilted but nonetheless characteristic sample of Mola's draughtsmanship, in which washes are used broadly to unify a design sketched in angular, abbreviated pen work.

PROVENANCE: Frank Jewett Mather, Jr. (Lugt 1853a).

EXHIBITIONS: New York, Roerich Museum, 1930, no. 74; New York, Durlacher Brothers, Italian Paintings and Drawings of the Seventeenth Century, 1932, no. 19 (as St. Peter in Prison).

Gift of Frank Jewett Mather, Jr., 52–167

55 *Studies for the Penitent St. Jerome*

Pen and brown ink, brown wash, on brown paper. 9⅟₁₆ × 8¹³⁄₁₆ inches (25.3 × 22.4 cm.). Brown stain at lower center.

Verso: Two studies of the penitent St. Jerome in pen and brown ink, brown and gray wash, over black chalk.

An excellent example of Mola's pen work at its freest and most energetic. A related study for the same composition with variations—the kneeling Jerome holds a book rather than a cross in his hands—is in the Teyler Museum at Haarlem (repr. J. Q. van Regteren Altena, *Les Dessins italiens de la Reine Christine de Suède*, Stockholm, 1966, pl. 99).

PROVENANCE: Richard Houlditch (Lugt 2214); Charles Fairfax Murray; sale, New York, Anderson Galleries, November 6–7, 1924, no. 294; Dan Fellows Platt (Lugt 2066b and 750a).

Bequest of Dan Fellows Platt, 48–760

SALVATOR ROSA

Naples 1615 – Rome 1673

56 *Studies for a Witches' Sabbath*

Pen and brown ink. 9 × 7⅜ inches (22.9 × 18.7 cm.). A number of oil spots on the sheet.

These rapid sketches of figures for a Witches' Sabbath are related in subject and style to a composition drawing in the Metropolitan Museum (repr. J. Bean, *100 European Drawings in The Metropolitan Museum of Art*, New York, 1964, pl. 36), which is probably a preparatory study for a picture in the Corsini collection in Florence, datable in the 1640s. Baldinucci records this commission: "Al marchese Bartolommeo Corsini dipinse un bel quadro d'incantesimi e stregonerie," a fine picture of incantations and witchcraft (F. Baldinucci, *La Vita di Salvatore Rosa*, Venetian edition of 1830, p. 56). Further drawings at Princeton (48–812 and 48–1271) and a sheet of studies in the Uffizi (12,102 F) can also be connected with the Corsini picture.

PROVENANCE: Dan Fellows Platt (Lugt 2066b and 750a), purchased by Platt from Parsons in 1929.

BIBLIOGRAPHY: Mahoney, *Rosa Drawings*, p. 192, no. 29.3.

Bequest of Dan Fellows Platt, 48–798

57 *Prometheus Bound*

Pen and brown ink, gray-brown wash. 9½ × 7¼ inches (24.2 × 18.5 cm.). Scattered mold spots. Lined.

Inscribed in pen and brown ink at lower margin, *Salvator Rosa*.

Verso: Illegible pen sketches, visible on recto.

Study for the Prometheus Bound, a picture datable in the 1650s, which once belonged to Rosa's principal patron, Carlo de' Rossi, and now is in the Galleria Nazionale d'Arte Antica in Rome (repr. *Pittori Napoletani del' 600 e del' 700*, Rome, Palazzo Barberini, 1958, fig. 38). There are variations between the picture and the drawing in the pose of the tortured figure of Prometheus, and in the picture the composition has been reversed. Mahoney lists five pen sketches in Leipzig (one reproduced in *Old Master Drawings*, VI, no. 24, March 1932, pl. 55), a drawing in the Farnesina and another in Budapest (repr. *Budapest Jahrbuch*, VI, 1931, p. 176, fig. 56) as studies for the Prometheus, in addition to the Princeton sheet. The persistent influence of Giuseppe Ribera on Rosa is apparent in the present drawing, not only in the dramatic treatment of the gruesome subject matter, but in the sparse and energetic pen work as well.

PROVENANCE: Dan Fellows Platt (Lugt 2066b and 750a), purchased by Platt in London in 1925.

BIBLIOGRAPHY: Walter Vitzthum, "Le Dessin baroque à Naples," *L'Oeil*, no. 97, January 1963, repr. p. 48; Mahoney, *Rosa Drawings*, p. 264, no. 43.3.

Bequest of Dan Fellows Platt, 48–799

58   *Studies for the Death of Regulus*

Pen and brown ink, brown wash. 8 ×9 ⅞ inches (20.3 ×25 cm.). Vertical fold at right. Partially lined.

Verso: Pen and brown ink study of a standing man pointing down, and of a leg.

Vitzhum was the first to point out that this is a study for the central group in Rosa's Death of Regulus, a picture now in the Museum at Richmond, Virginia (repr. Salerno, pl. 33, who dates the picture 1652 or shortly thereafter). The Roman consul Attilius Regulus was put to death by the Carthaginians who enclosed him in a barrel into which sharp spikes were driven. The figures on the left in the drawing are hammering in these spikes. The Louvre possesses a black chalk sketch for the horrified seated onlooker at the left of the composition (Inv. 9746, repr. Vitzthum, p. 74, fig. 37). Mahoney connects the figure study on the verso of this Princeton sheet with the 1652 Diogenes Discarding his Bowl, now in Copenhagen.

PROVENANCE: John MacGowan (Lugt 1496); Dan Fellows Platt (Lugt 750a), purchased by Platt from Parsons in 1929.

BIBLIOGRAPHY: Walter Vitzthum, "Seicento Drawings at the Cabinet des Dessins," *Burlington Magazine*, CII, 1960, p. 76, fig. 38; Luigi Salerno, *Salvator Rosa*, Florence, 1963, p. 122; Mahoney, *Rosa Drawings*, pp. 259–260, no. 42.1.

Bequest of Dan Fellows Platt, 48–610

59   *The Adoration of the Shepherds*

Black chalk. 9 ½×7 ⁷⁄₁₆ inches (24.1 ×18.9 cm.). Vertical crease at right of center. Lined.

Chalk drawings are fairly rare in Rosa's surviving production. The present fine example cannot be connected with a picture, but Mahoney dates it on stylistic grounds in the late 1650s, and relates it to two pen drawings of the same subject in Leipzig.

PROVENANCE: Dan Fellows Platt (Lugt 2066b and 750a), purchased by Platt from Parsons in 1929.

BIBLIOGRAPHY: Mahoney, *Rosa Drawings*, p. 325, no. 56.3.

Bequest of Dan Fellows Platt, 48–810

60 *Kneeling Figures*

Pen and brown ink, brown wash. 7$\frac{15}{16}$× 5$\frac{1}{2}$ inches (20.2×13.9 cm.). Triangular oil stain at lower right. Lined.

Handwriting on verso, not that of the artist, visible on recto.

Mahoney suggests that the kneeling figures studied on this sheet, as well as four further drawings at Princeton (48–791, 48–800, 48–1272, and 48–1279), are related to Rosa's picture representing the Angel Raphael Leaving the House of Tobit, datable in the early 1660s, now at Chantilly. A kneeling figure with hands raised in devotional wonder, probably Tobit himself, occupies the right foreground of the Chantilly composition. A further sheet of studies of kneeling figures, connectible with the picture, is in the Metropolitan Museum (38.179.1, purchased from the Platt collection; repr. *Art in Italy, 1600–1700*, Detroit Institute of Arts, 1965, p. 143). The Angel Leaving the House of Tobit is one of a group of religious subjects now at Chantilly that were painted by Rosa for Carlo de' Rossi; other subjects in the series are the Raising of Lazarus (see no. 61), Daniel in the Lion's Den, and Jeremiah Pulled Out of the Dungeon. The Jeremiah was exhibited in Rome at S. Giovanni Decollato in 1662, presumably shortly after the picture's completion.

PROVENANCE: Dan Fellows Platt (Lugt 2066b and 750a), purchased by Platt from Parsons in 1929.

BIBLIOGRAPHY: Mahoney, *Rosa Drawings*, p. 375, no. 66.18.

Bequest of Dan Fellows Platt, 49–71

61 *Studies of a Male Figure with Right Arm Raised, and of a Kneeling Female Figure*

Pen and brown ink, brown wash. 7$\frac{3}{4}$× 5$\frac{15}{16}$ inches (19.6×15.1 cm.). Lined.

Mahoney convincingly suggests that the male figure with arm raised in a gesture of command is a study for the miracle-working Christ, and the kneeling supplicating female a study for Lazarus's sister Mary in the Raising of Lazarus, a picture dating from the early 1660s now at Chantilly (repr. Luigi Salerno, *Salvator Rosa*, Florence, 1963, pl. 71). At Leipzig there are three pen sketches for the Chantilly picture, and a composition study is in the Metropolitan Museum (38.179.2, purchased from the Dan Fellows Platt collection).

PROVENANCE: Dan Fellows Platt (Lugt 2066b and 750a), purchased from Parsons in 1929.

BIBLIOGRAPHY: Mahoney, *Rosa Drawings*, pl. 369, no. 66.6.

Bequest of Dan Fellows Platt, 48–794

62 *Studies of an Executioner*

Pen and brown ink. 6$\frac{3}{8}$×8$\frac{1}{2}$ inches (16.2×21.6 cm.). Upper left and lower corners trimmed.

43

Verso: Two pen studies of a male figure with hands joined.

The studies for a scene of martyrdom by decapitation on the recto of this sheet, not related to a known picture by Rosa, are stylistically similar to, and no doubt contemporary with, the studies of a kneeling figure on the verso. Mahoney has connected the latter with the Martyrdom of Saints Cosmas and Damian, painted in 1669 for the Cappella Nerli in S. Giovanni dei Fiorentini in Rome.

PROVENANCE: Dan Fellows Platt (Lugt 2066b), purchased by Platt from Parsons in 1929.

BIBLIOGRAPHY: Mahoney, *Rosa Drawings*, p. 465, no. 85.6.

Bequest of Dan Fellows Platt, 48–804

63 *Youth Pulling off His Shirt, Full Figure*

Pen and brown ink, brown wash. 3$\frac{13}{16}$ × 2$\frac{1}{2}$ inches (9.7 × 6.4 cm.). Lined.

Like no. 64 below, another study of a youth pulling off his shirt, this drawing cannot be connected with a surviving picture by Rosa. The figure would be appropriate in a Baptism scene, or in a landscape with bathers similar to the fine example at the Yale University Art Gallery (repr. Luigi Salerno, *Salvator Rosa*, Florence, 1963, fig. 48a). The figure style in both drawings is that of Rosa's maturity.

PROVENANCE: Dan Fellows Platt (Lugt 2066b and 750a), purchased by Platt from Parsons in 1929.

BIBLIOGRAPHY: Walter Vitzthum, "Le Dessin baroque à Naples," *L'Oeil*, no. 97,

January 1963, repr. p. 51; Mahoney, *Rosa Drawings*, p. 392, no. 69.2.

Bequest of Dan Fellows Platt, 48–1274

64 *Youth Pulling off His Shirt, Half Figure*

Pen and brown ink, brown wash. 2$\frac{9}{16}$ × 2$\frac{1}{4}$ inches (6.5 × 5.7 cm.). Lined.

See no. 63 above.

PROVENANCE: Dan Fellows Platt (Lugt 2066b and 750a), purchased by Platt from Parsons in 1929.

BIBLIOGRAPHY: Mahoney, *Rosa Drawings*, p. 393, no. 69.3.

Bequest of Dan Fellows Platt, 48–1275

DOMENICO PIOLA

Genoa 1627 – Genoa 1703

65 *Three Seated Female Figures, Two Putti, and a Dog*

Pen and brown ink, brown wash, over black chalk. 10$\frac{9}{16}$ × 7$\frac{3}{8}$ inches (26.8 × 18.8 cm.). Lined.

Inscribed in pen and brown ink at lower right corner, *1676*.

Formerly classified as Italian anonymous, but certainly the work of Domenico Piola, this sheet contains studies made with one of his many decorative commissions in mind.

PROVENANCE: Dan Fellows Platt (Lugt 2066b and 750a), purchased by Platt from Meatyard in 1925.

Bequest of Dan Fellows Platt, 48–580

66 *Madonna and Child with the Infant Baptist*

Pen and brown ink, brown wash, over black chalk. 8 15/16 × 6 1/16 inches (22.7 × 15.4 cm.). Lined.

Good example of the work of this enormously productive Genoese draughtsman.

PROVENANCE: Dan Fellows Platt (Lugt 2066b and 750a), purchased by Platt from Ederheimer in 1924.

Bequest of Dan Fellows Platt, 48–774

CIRO FERRI

Rome 1634 – Rome 1689

67 *The Martyrdom of St. Bibiana*

Black chalk on light brownish paper. 9 13/16 × 13 3/8 inches (24.9 × 33.9 cm.). Lined.

Inscribed in pen and brown ink at lower right, *7 [?] 8.*

The drawing is traditionally attributed to Pietro da Cortona, and indeed it is a free copy of Cortona's early fresco representing the Martyrdom of St. Bibiana in the nave of S. Bibiana in Rome (repr. Giuliano Briganti, *Pietro da Cortona*, Rome, 1962, pl. 36). Walter Vitzthum was the first to point out in a note on the mount that the sheet is a characteristic example of the chalk draughtsmanship of Cortona's diligent pupil and assistant, Ciro Ferri. Vitzthum further has called attention to a fairly exact replica, probably a copy, of the Princeton drawing in the Museum at Lille (Henry Pluchart, *Ville de Lille. Musée Wicar. Notice des dessins . . .*, Lille, 1889, p. 49, no. 242, as Ciro Ferri; Gernsheim photograph no. 18080).

PROVENANCE: Frank Jewett Mather, Jr., purchased by Mather from Coffin in Worcester, Massachusetts.

Gift of Frank Jewett Mather, Jr., 45–70

CESARE GENNARI

Cento 1637 – Bologna 1688

68 *Caricature of a Man in a Turban Holding a Pestle*

Pen and brown ink. 5 13/16 × 5 9/16 inches (14.8 × 14.1 cm.).

Signed in pen and brown ink on verso, *Cesare Genari f Il di . . . 1671.A.° FA:.*

The signature and date on the verso of this sheet make it a useful touchstone for the pen style of Cesare Gennari, whose manner owes so much to, but by its very hesitancy is clearly distinguishable from, that of his uncle, Guercino. It will be noted that the sheet is dated 1671, i.e., five years after Guercino's death.

PROVENANCE: Dan Fellows Platt (Lugt 2066b and 750a).

Bequest of Dan Fellows Platt, 48–690

GIOVANNI BATTISTA GAULLI, called BACICCIO, Attributed to

Genoa 1639 – Rome 1709

69 *The Flood*

Pen and brown ink, brown wash, heightened with white, on blue-green paper. 9 × 13 13/16 inches (22.9 × 35.1 cm.). Lined.

Inscribed in pen and brown ink at lower left, *Grimaldi*; on verso in black chalk at center, *Bacicio*.

Inscribed with the name of Grimaldi and assigned to this Bolognese artist in the Princeton inventory, the drawing is related stylistically and by its subject matter to three others, all of which emanate from the circle of Gian Lorenzo Bernini and are possibly, even probably, the work Bernini's Genoese-born protégé, Giovanni Battista Gaulli. Two of these drawings, of horizontal format like the Princeton sheet, are in the Louvre. They represent God the Father Appearing to Adam and Eve, and an Episode from the Flood (Inv. 9572 and 9573 as Bernini; *Musée du Louvre. Dessins romains du XVIIe siècle*, 1959, nos. 19 and 20, respectively, attributed with reservation to Bernini). The Louvre drawings come from the collection of Pierre-Jean Mariette, who considered them to be the work of Bernini, and indeed they show a striking formal dependence on Bernini's sculptural style and draughtsmanship. This very dependence suggests that the young Gaulli might be the author of the Louvre drawings, for Bernini himself must be excluded. That Mariette, on another occasion, confused Bernini and Gaulli has been pointed out; a drawing in the Morgan Library (repr. C. Fairfax Murray, *Drawings by the Old Masters, Collection of J. Pierpont Morgan* IV, London, no. 177) was attributed by Mariette to Bernini, but is in fact a typical Gaulli (H. Brauer and R. Wittkower, *Die Zeichnungen des Gianlorenzo Bernini*, I, Berlin, 1931, p. 154, note 2, also W. Vitzthum, *Burlington Magazine*, CII, 1960, p. 76). The St. Louis Museum

possesses the fourth drawing in the series. It is a horizontal composition representing Adam Tempted by Eve (no. 26:49; with an old, partially effaced inscription, *Baciccio*). There is a progressive decline in quality from the Louvre drawings through the Princeton sheet to the St. Louis drawing, and the latter may be an old copy. Nonetheless, they form a reasonably coherent group of representations of Old Testament subjects that can be attributed with some confidence to the young Gaulli, strongly influenced by Bernini. It should be further observed that the present drawing has an old attribution to Baciccio inscribed on the verso.

PROVENANCE: Purchased by The Art Museum from Delius Giese in New York in 1955.

Laura P. Hall Memorial Fund, 55–1

DONATO CRETI
Cremona 1671 – Bologna 1749

70 *Studies for Jacob Wrestling with the Angel*

Pen and brown ink. $8\frac{1}{2} \times 9\frac{9}{16}$ inches (21.6 × 24.3 cm.). Lined.

These sketches, in which the light, nervous pen work is so characteristic of Creti, were very probably made in preparation for a picture representing Jacob Wrestling with the Angel, now in the Casa del Clero in Bologna. Renato Roli, who recently published the picture, pointed out that it may be identical with a painting of the same subject mentioned by Giovanni Pietro Zanotti as commissioned by the Bolognese Cardinal Davia (R. Roli, "Dipinti inediti di Donato Creti," *Arte Antica e Moderna*, no. 23, 1963, p. 251, fig. 108 c).

PROVENANCE: Archduke Friedrich of Austria (according to pencil inscription on verso of former mount); Mathias Komor, New York; Nathan V. Hammer, purchased by Hammer from Komor in 1955.

Gift of Nathan V. Hammer, 59–34

MARCO RICCI
Belluno 1676 – Venice 1729

71 *Pilgrims Resting*

Pen and brown ink. 15¾×13½ inches (40×34.3 cm.). Framing lines in pen and brown ink, brush and blue water color drawn on the original sheet.

Signed in pen and brown ink at lower left, *Marco Ricci*.

An excellent example of Marco Ricci's pen draughtsmanship, bold and coarse, yet remarkably effective. The framing lines drawn on the sheet are no doubt by the artist himself, who broke off his design at the top of the sheet in order to leave place for the drawn fillets. A stylistically very similar signed drawing by Marco Ricci in the Fogg Museum, representing three men resting near a pyramid, has comparable framing lines drawn on the sheet itself (Agnes Mongan and Paul J. Sachs, *Drawings in the Fogg Museum of Art*, Cambridge, Massachusetts, 1940, I, p. 171, no. 345; II, fig. 170, the framing lines not reproduced), as does a related pen drawing in the British Museum (1936–10–10–14) of a pilgrim displaying a figure of the Virgin to kneeling figures.

PROVENANCE: Dan Fellows Platt (Lugt 750a).

BIBLIOGRAPHY: Benesch, *Venetian Drawings*, p. 27, pl. 3.

Bequest of Dan Fellows Platt, 48–778

ALESSANDRO MAGNASCO
Genoa 1677 – Genoa 1749

72 *Penitent Monk*

Brush and black ink, gray wash, heightened with white, over black chalk, on brown paper. 11½×6⅞ inches (29.2×17.5 cm.).

Verso: Figure studies in black chalk, brown wash, and white.

A somewhat smaller but very similar design, without the arched top of the present sheet, is in the Hamburg Kunsthalle (repr. Benno Geiger, *I Disegni del Magnasco*, Padua, 1945, pl. 108). Both versions appear to be autograph, and one is not surprised to find Magnasco repeating such a very characteristic monkish figure.

PROVENANCE: Dan Fellows Platt.

Bequest of Dan Fellows Platt, 47–82

GIOVANNI BATTISTA PIAZZETTA
Venice 1682 – Venice 1754

73 *Head of a Woman*

Black and white chalk on brownish paper. 14⁵⁄₁₆×10³⁄₁₆ inches (36.4×25.9 cm.). A number of repaired losses. Sheet considerably foxed. Lined.

A typical Piazzetta head study, somewhat damaged, but of good quality.

PROVENANCE: Dan Fellows Platt (Lugt 750a).

Bequest of Dan Fellows Platt, 48–768

GASPARO DIZIANI

Belluno 1689 – Venice 1767

74   *Apollo and Marsyas*

Pen and brown ink, brown wash, over a little black chalk. $9\frac{1}{2} \times 11\frac{5}{8}$ inches (24.1 ×29.6 cm.).

This drawing came to The Art Museum from the Platt collection with an unconvincing attribution to the French sculptor Augustin Pajou, and it has been published as the work of Pajou by Benisovich. However, the bravura draughtsmanship is clearly Venetian, not French, and it is more than probable that the drawing is the work of the enormously prolific Gasparo Diziani. The rather angular and abbreviated figure style is unmistakably his, and may be compared with many examples of Diziani's draughtsmanship in the Museo Correr in Venice, which possesses the largest and best-documented collection of his drawings.

PROVENANCE: Dan Fellows Platt (Lugt 750a).

BIBLIOGRAPHY: Michel N. Benisovich, "Drawings by the Sculptor Augustin Pajou in The Art Museum," *Record of The Art Museum. Princeton University*, XIV, no. 1, 1955, p. 15, fig. 6.

Bequest of Dan Fellows Platt, 48–395

GIOVANNI BATTISTA TIEPOLO

Venice 1696 – Madrid 1770

75   *Soldier*

Red chalk and red wash, over a little black chalk. $10\frac{5}{16} \times 7\frac{1}{8}$ inches (26.2 ×18.1 cm.).

Inscribed in pen and brown ink at lower right corner, *Tiepolo fece.*

The rather hesitant contours, the flickering contrasts of light and shade, and the use of red chalk washed with water in this drawing connect it with a group of figure studies that are generally considered to be among Giambattista Tiepolo's earliest surviving drawings, probably datable well before 1730. Other examples in this style and technique are at Udine, Wellesley College, Bassano (repr. Rizzi, pls. 4, 5, and 6 respectively), in London (repr. George Knox, *Catalogue of the Tiepolo Drawings in the Victoria and Albert Museum*, London, 1960, no. 3) and Stockholm. Knox calls attention to another related example, a study of two flying angels, now in Count Seilern's collection, which, like the present sheet, formerly belonged to Dan Fellows Platt (sold London, Sotheby's, October 21, 1963, no. 161).

PROVENANCE: Count Algarotti, Venice (according to pencil inscription on verso); Dan Fellows Platt (Lugt 2066b and 750a), purchased by Platt from Parsons in 1923.

BIBLIOGRAPHY: Knox, *Princeton Record*, 1964, p. 8, no. 1, repr. p. 1 and p. 12; A. Rizzi, *Disegni del Tiepolo. Catalogo della Mostra*, Udine, 1965, p. 54.

Bequest of Dan Fellows Platt, 48–842

76 *Faith, Hope, and Charity*

Pen and brown ink, brown and gray wash, heightened with white, over traces of black chalk. 15 $\frac{7}{16}$ × 10 $\frac{3}{16}$ inches (39.2 × 25.9 cm.).

This highly finished drawing, probably made for sale or presentation, is one of a group of early Giambattista Tiepolo designs that came into the possession of the Venetian engraver Pietro Monaco (1707–1772). Eight such religious compositions, including the present sheet, were engraved by Monaco and published, probably in 1739, with captions indicating that they then belonged to the engraver himself. George Knox has identified four of the eight drawings that Monaco possessed and engraved; in addition to the present sheet, drawings now in the Art Institute of Chicago, the Civico Museo Correr in Venice, and the Museo Civico at Bassano served as models for Monaco's prints, while four of the original drawings have yet to be rediscovered. Knox suggests a general dating between 1625 and 1632 for these elaborate designs.

PROVENANCE: Dan Fellows Platt (Lugt 2066b and 750a), purchased by Platt from Meatyard in 1928.

BIBLIOGRAPHY: Benesch, *Venetian Drawings*, p. 30, pl. 13; Knox, *Princeton Record*, 1964, p. 25, no. 58, repr. p. 18; George Knox, "A Group of Tiepolo Drawings Owned and Engraved by Pietro Monaco," *Master Drawings*, III, 1965, no. 4, p. 392, pl. 30.

Bequest of Dan Fellows Platt, 48–770

77 *Prudence and a River God*

Pen and brown ink, gray wash, over black chalk. 7 $\frac{3}{8}$ × 6 $\frac{1}{2}$ inches (18.8 × 16.6 cm.).

On stylistic grounds Knox associates this drawing with Tiepolo's studies for the decoration of the Villa Loschi at Biron near Vicenza, though these figures do not occur in the frescoes, which date from 1734.

PROVENANCE: Count Algarotti, Venice (according to pencil inscription on verso of drawing); Dan Fellows Platt (Lugt 750a), purchased by Platt from Parsons in 1922.

BIBLIOGRAPHY: Knox, *Princeton Record*, 1964, p. 8, no. 2, repr. p. 12.

Bequest of Dan Fellows Platt, 48–885

78 *Male and Female Fauns*

Pen and brown ink, brown wash, over traces of black chalk. 11 $\frac{1}{8}$ × 14 $\frac{3}{16}$ inches (28.3 × 36.1 cm.). Several brown stains at upper left. Lined.

In style, subject matter, and dimensions this drawing is related to, and was very probably part of, a series of drawings connected with Giambattista's frescoes of 1740 in the Palazzo Clerici in Milan. The series, now divided between the Metropolitan Museum, the Morgan Library, and the Horne Foundation in Florence, includes figure studies used in the ceiling. The two figures in the Princeton group do not, however, appear in the fresco, but the same seated nymph is used again in one of the Clerici drawings in the Metropolitan Museum (37.165.36).

PROVENANCE: Arthur Frothingham; Frank Jewett Mather, Jr. (Lugt 1853a).

BIBLIOGRAPHY: Ulrich Middeldorf, *Print Collector's Quarterly*, XXV, 1938, repr. p. 104; Knox, *Princeton Record*, 1964, p. 8, no. 4, repr. p. 12.

EXHIBITIONS: Lawrence, The University of Kansas Museum of Art, Masterworks from University and College Art Collections, 1958, no. 64; Newark, The Newark Museum, Old Master Drawings, 1960, no. 54, repr.

Gift of Frank Jewett Mather, Jr., 44–18

79 *Seated Virgin and Child*

Pen and brown ink on light brown paper. 6 × 5 ¼ inches (15.2 × 13.3 cm.).

Verso: Pen and brown ink figure studies.

This hasty sketch of the Virgin seen in steep perspective is, as Mras has pointed out, a study related to a painted model for the now destroyed ceiling of the Chiesa degli Scalzi in Venice, where the Virgin appears seated on the roof of the Holy House of Loreto (the *modello* repr. Antonio Morassi, *A Complete Catalogue of the Paintings of Tiepolo*, London, 1962, fig. 87, dated about 1743). Another pen sketch at Princeton, where the Virgin conspicuously holds the Child Jesus in her right arm (44–882, repr. Mras, *Princeton Record*, 1956, p. 43, fig. 4), can be related to another model for the Scalzi ceiling in the Rosebery collection (Morassi, *op. cit.*, fig. 88) where, as in the fresco, the Christ Child in the Virgin's arms is a prominent feature of the design.

PROVENANCE: Count Algarotti, Venice (according to pencil inscription on old mount); Dan Fellows Platt (Lugt 750a), purchased by Platt from Parsons in 1927.

BIBLIOGRAPHY: Mras, *Princeton Record*, 1956, pp. 40–44, fig. 1; Knox, *Princeton Record*, 1964, p. 8, no. 7, repr. p. 12.

Bequest of Dan Fellows Platt, 48–868

80 *St. Paulinus Exorcising a Possessed Boy*

Pen, brown and black ink, gray-brown wash, over black chalk. 12 × 8 $\frac{13}{16}$ inches (30.4 × 22.4 cm.).

This brilliant sketch and the equally energetic nos. 81 and 82 below represent the early stages of Giambattista's planning of an altarpiece datable about 1746, representing St. Paulinus of Aquilea Exorcising, painted for the church of S. Giovanni di Verdara, and now in the Museo Civico at Padua (Antonio Morassi, *A Complete Catalogue of the Paintings of Tiepolo*, London, 1962, fig. 153, wrongly described as a Miracle of St. Patrick). The various solutions for the gestures of St. Paulinus proposed in the Princeton drawings, first connected with the Padua altarpiece by Mras, were not retained by Tiepolo in the picture, where the preacher facing forward raises his left arm in admonition. Further preparatory studies at the Fitzwilliam Museum in Cambridge (repr. Rizzi, pls. 83 and 84), the Hermitage in Leningrad (repr. L. Salmina, *Disegni veneti del Museo di Leningrado*, Venice, 1964, pl. 68), and in Count Seilern's collection in London are closer to the finished altarpiece. This series of drawings provides as Knox remarks, "an admirable account of the development of a Tiepolo composition. Against the great commissions of the middle forties, the altarpiece of our inconspicuous Paduan church might appear a matter of secondary importance for the Tiepolo workshop. The drawings show the careful consideration it received, and the turbulent creative process that lies behind the calm precision of the completed work."

The composition is sometimes described as St. Paulinus preaching, but in fact it represents the saint exorcising a boy possessed by the devil.

PROVENANCE: Bellingham Smith (according to pencil inscription on verso); Dan Fellows Platt (Lugt 2066b and 750a), purchased by Platt from William Patterson in 1928.

BIBLIOGRAPHY: Mras, *Princeton Record*, 1956, pp. 44–50, fig. 9; Knox, *Princeton Record*, 1964, pp. 8–9, nos. 8, 9, and 10, repr. p. 12; A. Rizzi, *Disegni del Tiepolo. Catalogo della Mostra*, Udine, 1965, p. 100.

Bequest of Dan Fellows Platt, 48–869

81 St. Paulinus Exorcising a Possessed Boy

Pen, brown and black ink, gray-brown wash, over black chalk. $12\frac{1}{8} \times 8\frac{3}{4}$ inches (30.8 ×22.2 cm.). All four corners of sheet trimmed. Lined.

See no. 80 above.

PROVENANCE: Parsons, London; Dan Fellows Platt (Lugt 2066b and 750a), purchased by Platt from Weyhe in 1924.

BIBLIOGRAPHY: See no. 80 above.

Bequest of Dan Fellows Platt, 48–875

82 St. Paulinus Exorcising a Possessed Boy

Pen, brown and black ink, gray-brown wash, over traces of black chalk. $12 \times 8\frac{9}{16}$ inches (30.5 ×21.7 cm.). Lined.

See no. 80 above.

PROVENANCE: Count Algarotti, Venice (according to pencil inscription on mat); Dan Fellows Platt (Lugt 2066b and 750a), purchased by Platt from Parsons in 1924.

BIBLIOGRAPHY: See no. 80 above.

Bequest of Dan Fellows Platt, 48–876

83 Roger Mounted on a Hippogriff

Pen and brown ink, brown wash, over black chalk. $5\frac{3}{8} \times 6\frac{7}{8}$ inches (13.7 × 17.5 cm.). All four corners of sheet trimmed. Lined.

Knox identified this drawing as a study for the fresco representing the Liberation of Angelica by Roger, painted by Giambattista in 1757 on the walls of the Ariosto Room in the Villa Valmarana near Vicenza (repr. R. Pallucchini, *Gli Affreschi di Giambattista e Giandomenico Tiepolo alla Villa Valmarana*, Bergamo, 1944, pl. 38). A pen and wash drawing for the Angelica and Medor fresco on another wall of the room is in London (repr. Knox, *Victoria and Albert Catalogue*, no. 249).

PROVENANCE: Count Algarotti, Venice (according to pencil inscription on verso of old mount); Dan Fellows Platt (Lugt 750a), purchased by Platt from Parsons in 1926.

BIBLIOGRAPHY: George Knox, *Catalogue of the Tiepolo Drawings in the Victoria and Albert Museum*, London, 1960, p. 83;

Knox, *Princeton Record*, 1964, p. 24, no. 53, repr. p. 17.

Bequest of Dan Fellows Platt, 48–843

84 *Study for Faith, Hope, and Charity*

Pen and brown ink on light brown paper. 6⅜×5⅝ inches (16.2×14.3 cm.).

George Mras has convincingly identified this drawing as a study for the group representing Faith, Hope, and Charity on the frescoed ceiling in the Throne Room of the Royal Palace in Madrid, executed by Giambattista and his assistants between 1762 and 1764 (Antonio Morassi, *G. B. Tiepolo. His Life and His Work*, London, 1955, pl. 82). In the fresco Faith carries the cross at her left side, Charity, holding an infant, appears at the right, and Hope with her anchor is moved forward. In style the drawing corresponds with two sketches in London that are connectible with the Madrid ceiling (repr. George Knox, *Catalogue of the Tiepolo Drawings in the Victoria and Albert Museum*, London, 1960, nos. 302 and 303). The London sketches were inserted in an album assembled by Tiepolo before his departure for Madrid in April 1762. In March of that year he was already at work on plans for decorations of the Throne Room, and this Princeton sheet as well as the two London drawings were probably made in Venice rather than Madrid.

PROVENANCE: Dan Fellows Platt (Lugt 750a), purchased by Platt from Holoway in 1924.

BIBLIOGRAPHY: Mras, *Princeton Record*, 1956, pp. 53–54, fig. 17; Knox, *Princeton Record*, 1964, p. 25, no. 57, repr. p. 18.

Bequest of Dan Fellows Platt, 48–881

85 *Head, after a Bust of Palma Giovane by Alessandro Vittoria*

Red chalk, heightened with white, on blue paper. 9¹³⁄₁₆×7¹⁄₁₆ inches (24.9×17.9 cm.).

Inscribed on verso in pen and brown ink, *Disegno di G. B. Tiepolo Veneto.*

A version of Alessandro Vittoria's bust of the sixteenth-century Venetian painter Palma Giovane must have been available in the Tiepolo studio, for a number of Tiepolesque chalk drawings after this head, seen from various angles, exist. Some of the drawings, like the present sheet, are by Giambattista himself, as are examples in the Rasini collection in Milan (repr. Antonio Morassi, *G. B. Tiepolo. His Life and His Work*, London, 1955, pl. 39), in the British Museum (1869–4–10–2490), and formerly in the Wendland collection (repr. K. T. Parker, *Old Master Drawings*, IX, 1935, p. 62). A copy after the bust in the Ashmolean Museum in Oxford has been attributed to Lorenzo Tiepolo; it was on the occasion of the publication of the Oxford drawing that K. T. Parker (*op. cit.*, pp. 61–63) identified the common model of the whole group as the Vittoria bust. The Princeton sheet was first associated with it by Fröhlich-Bume.

PROVENANCE: Private collection, Vienna; Frank Jewett Mather, Jr. (Lugt 1853a).

BIBLIOGRAPHY: L. Fröhlich-Bume, "Notes on Some Works by Giovanni Battista Tiepolo," *Burlington Magazine*, LXXII, 1938, p. 87, pl. 1c; Mras, *Princeton Record*, 1956, p. 58, fig. 20; Knox, *Princeton Record*, 1964, pp. 9–10, no. 11, repr. p. 12.

Gift of Frank Jewett Mather, Jr., 44–15

86 *Walking Man, Back View*

Pen and brown ink, brown wash. 8½×
5¾ inches (21.6×14.7 cm.).

Dan Fellows Platt acquired at least twenty-six Giambattista Tiepolo studies of single standing draped figures from one of the three albums of Tiepolo drawings bought by Parsons at Christie's in 1914. Knox points out that this series of single figures may have formed a volume very similar in character to the album of Giambattista's drawings in the Victoria and Albert Museum labeled *Sole Figure Vestite T: I:.* Of Platt's considerable group of these charming exercises in figure drawing seven (see also nos. 87 and 88 below) came to Princeton in his bequest, while the rest were dispersed in America. The present example and the two below testify to the stylistic consistency of the series.

PROVENANCE: Edward Cheney (?); Dan Fellows Platt (Lugt 750a), purchased by Platt from Parsons.

BIBLIOGRAPHY: Benesch, *Venetian Drawings*, p. 34, pl. 37; Knox, *Princeton Record*, 1964, p. 10, no. 13, repr. p. 13.

87 *Man in Turban*

Pen and brown ink, brown wash. 8⅝×
5¹³⁄₁₆ inches (21.9×14.8 cm.).

Verso: Illegible black chalk sketches.

See no. 86 above.

PROVENANCE: Count Algarotti, Venice (according to pencil inscription on mat); Edward Cheney (?); Dan Fellows Platt (Lugt 750a), purchased by Platt from Parsons in 1925.

BIBLIOGRAPHY: Knox, *Princeton Record*, 1964, p. 10, no. 14, repr. p. 13.

Bequest of Dan Fellows Platt, 48–859

88 *Standing Man, Frontal*

Pen and brown ink, brown wash, on light brown paper. 8¹³⁄₁₆×5⁷⁄₁₆ inches (22.4×13.8 cm.).

See no. 86 above.

PROVENANCE: Count Algarotti, Venice (according to pencil inscription on mat); Edward Cheney (?); Dan Fellows Platt (Lugt 750a), purchased by Platt from Parsons in 1920.

BIBLIOGRAPHY: Knox, *Princeton Record*, 1964, p. 10, no. 17, repr. p. 13.

Bequest of Dan Fellows Platt, 48–862

89 *Woman Holding Platter*

Pen and brown ink, brown wash. 10⁷⁄₁₆×
7½ inches (26.5×19 cm.). Lower left corner trimmed.

Inscribed in pen and gray ink at lower left corner, *109.*

Verso: Two pen and brown ink studies of a draped figure.

This drawing and nos. 90–94 below are part of a series of twenty-four sketches of single figures, seen in steep perspective from below, which came to Princeton in the bequest of Dan Fellows Platt. Others in the series had been sold from the Platt collection before 1948. Most of these drawings were acquired by Platt from Parsons in London between 1922 and 1926, and they all presumably came from an album labeled *Sole Figure per Soffitti* (once probably in Edward Cheney's collection, as Knox has suggested) that was sold with two others at Christie's, July 14, 1914. The albums were purchased by Parsons and, at the end of World War I, broken up, and the drawings (a total of some three hundred in the three volumes) offered for sale individually. The contents of the album *Sole Figure per Soffitti* are now widely scattered over Europe and America, but Platt appears to have obtained the lion's share of the drawings. They must have formed a complete repertory, a kind of pattern book, recording poses for figures seated or standing on clouds; the sketches were probably made with no particular scheme in mind, but might be drawn upon when a ceiling decoration was undertaken by the studio. It would be difficult to date these drawings, though they are certainly the work of the mature Giambattista, and no one of them seems to be a preparatory study for a specific figure in any ceiling decoration. George Mras has pointed out connections with the ceiling fresco in the Villa Pisani at Strà in two cases (see no. 91), but Knox remarks that "these relationships may go no further than that the ceiling contains recollections of the drawings" (*Princeton Record*, 1964, p. 6).

PROVENANCE: Count Algarotti, Venice (according to pencil inscription on verso of mount); Edward Cheney (?); Dan Fellows Platt (Lugt 750a), purchased by Platt from Parsons in 1922.

BIBLIOGRAPHY: Knox, *Princeton Record*, 1964, p. 11, no. 20, repr. p. 13.

Bequest of Dan Fellows Platt, 48–831

90 *Seated Figure, Arms Raised*

Pen and brown ink, gray wash. $6\frac{3}{16} \times 5\frac{9}{16}$ inches (15.7 × 14.1 cm.).

See no. 89 above.

PROVENANCE: Count Algarotti, Venice (according to pencil inscription on mat); Edward Cheney (?); Dan Fellows Platt (Lugt 750a), purchased by Platt from Parsons in 1922.

BIBLIOGRAPHY: Knox, *Princeton Record*, 1964, p. 11, no. 24, repr. p. 14.

Bequest of Dan Fellows Platt, 48–835

91 *Seated Figure, Hand to Head*

Pen and brown ink, brown wash. $8\frac{1}{2} \times 6\frac{7}{16}$ inches (21.6 × 16.4 cm.).

See no. 89 above. Mras has suggested a connection with the ceiling fresco executed in 1761–1762 at the Villa Pisani at Strà, where a similar figure appears in a corner of the vast composition.

PROVENANCE: Count Algarotti, Venice (according to pencil inscription on mat); Edward Cheney (?); Dan Fellows Platt (Lugt 750a), purchased by Platt from Parsons in 1924.

BIBLIOGRAPHY: Mras, *Princeton Record*, 1956, pp. 50–51, fig. 12; Knox, *Princeton Record*, 1964, p. 11, no. 26, repr. p. 14.

Bequest of Dan Fellows Platt, 48–837

92 *Reclining Youth with Staff*

Pen and brown ink, brown wash. $8\frac{1}{8} \times 6\frac{1}{4}$ inches (20.6 × 15.9 cm.).

See no. 89 above.

PROVENANCE: Edward Cheney (?); Dan Fellows Platt (Lugt 750a).

BIBLIOGRAPHY: *Allen Memorial Art Museum Bulletin, Oberlin College*, VIII, no. 2,

Winter 1951, p. 57, no. 20, pl. 20; Knox, *Princeton Record*, 1964, p. 11, no. 35, repr. p. 15.

Bequest of Dan Fellows Platt, 48–850

93   *Figure Striding, Holding Knee*

Pen and brown ink, brown wash. 10½× 7¹¹⁄₁₆ inches (26.7×19.5 cm.).

Inscribed in pen and gray ink at lower left corner, *27*.

Verso: Pen and brown ink study for the same figure.

See no. 89 above.

PROVENANCE: Count Algarotti, Venice (according to pencil inscription on mat); Edward Cheney (?); Dan Fellows Platt (Lugt 750a), purchased by Platt from Parsons in 1923.

BIBLIOGRAPHY: Knox, *Princeton Record*, 1964, p. 22, no. 39, repr. p. 16.

Bequest of Dan Fellows Platt, 48–854

94   *Female Figure, Right Arm Raised*

Pen and brown ink, brown wash, on light brown paper. 9¾×6¹³⁄₁₆ inches (24.7× 17.3 cm.).

See no. 89 above.

PROVENANCE: Count Algarotti, Venice (according to pencil inscription on mat); Dan Fellows Platt (Lugt 750a), purchased by Platt from Parsons in 1923.

BIBLIOGRAPHY: Knox, *Princeton Record*, 1964, p. 22, no. 40, repr. p. 16.

Bequest of Dan Fellows Platt, 48–855

95   *Male Head, Profile to Left*

Pen and brown ink, brown wash, over black chalk. 9⅞×7¹³⁄₁₆ inches (25.1×19.8 cm.). Spot at lower left.

Inscribed in pen and gray ink in lower left corner, *60*.

This drawing was one of some sixty Giambattista Tiepolo heads in an album dispersed by the Savile Gallery in London in 1928. A handwritten note in the Savile album by the collector Edward Cheney, who owned the great block of Giambattista's sketches now in the Victoria and Albert Museum, recorded the provenance of the volume: *This collection was made by G. B. Tiepolo himself and given by him and his son for the Library of the Sommasco convent (S. Maria della Salute) at Venice in which he was professed. At the suppression of the convents the volumes fell into the hands of Cicognara by whom they were given in an exchange to Canova from whom they passed after his death to Mons. [?] Canova his brother, by him they were sold to Sigr. Francesco Pesaro and by him to me. E. C. Venice, 1842.*
  Princeton possesses another head study from the Savile album (no. 53–62).

PROVENANCE: S. Maria della Salute, Venice; Cicognara; Canova, Venice, 1822; Pesaro; Edward Cheney; Savile Gallery, London; Richard Owen, Paris; private collection, Washington; sale, Parke-Bernet, New York, January 17–19, 1952, lot no. 264, with Princeton 53–62.

BIBLIOGRAPHY: Knox, *Princeton Record*, 1964, p. 23, no. 45, repr. p. 16.

Laura P. Hall Memorial Fund, 53–63

POMPEO GIROLAMO BATONI
Lucca 1708 – Rome 1787

96 *Sleeping Christ Child*

Red chalk, heightened with white, on brown-washed paper; squared in red chalk. 8⅝×11⅞ inches (21.9×30.2 cm.). Lined.

In 1932 Emmerling connected this drawing, which then belonged to Hermann Voss, with Batoni's Holy Family at Pommersfelden, where the sleeping Christ Child is seen in reverse and in a slightly different position (repr. Emmerling, no. 90). Anthony Clark points out, however, that the drawing is Batoni's exact and painstaking study for the sleeping Child in a Holy Family in the Merenda collection at Forlì (repr. *Emporium*, XCIX, 1944, p. 99, fig. 3; CXII, 1953, p. 58). Mr. Clark himself possesses two further studies for the Forlì picture, which dates from the 1740s: a study of the Christ Child and of drapery, also from Voss's collection (Emmerling, z.13,2), and a signed study for the figure of St. Joseph.

PROVENANCE: Hermann Voss; Mathias Komor; Nathan V. Hammer, purchased by Hammer from Komor in New York in 1955.

BIBLIOGRAPHY: Ernst Emmerling, *Pompeo Batoni, sein Leben und Werk*, Darmstadt, 1932, p. 141, z.13,1.

Gift of Nathan V. Hammer, 59–35

FRANCESCO FONTEBASSO
Venice 1709 – Venice 1768/1769

97 *Nymphs in a Landscape*

Pen and brown ink, over a little black chalk. 10½×14¾ inches (26.8×37.4 cm.). Red chalk lines at upper right, not related to the design. Lined.

This drawing, as Byam Shaw has pointed out, is Fontebasso's study for one of his rare original engravings (A. De Vesme, *Le Peintre-graveur italien*, Milan, 1906, p. 476, no. 6). The engraved composition, of the same dimensions as the drawing but in reverse, is part of a series of eight mythological subjects. Impressions of the series in the Dresden Kupferstichkabinett have a title page reading *Varii Baccanali et Istorie Inventate et Incise in Rame dal Signor Francesco Fontebasso Celebre Pittore Veneto*, and dated 1744.

PROVENANCE: Frank Jewett Mather, Jr.

BIBLIOGRAPHY: Benesch, *Venetian Drawings*, p. 28, pl. 5; John [sic] Scholz, "Notes on Drawings by Francesco Fontebasso," *L'Arte*, XVIII, n.s., 1948–1951, pp. 41–42, fig. 3 (wrongly described in the caption as in the Scholz collection); J. Byam Shaw, "The Drawings of Francesco Fontebasso," *Arte Veneta*, VIII, 1954, p. 323.

Gift of Frank Jewett Mather, Jr., 46–1

98 *Studies of Nude Male Figures*

Pen and ink, brown and gray wash, over black chalk. 14⅞×10⁷⁄₁₆ inches (37.8×26.5 cm.). Vertical ruled lines at left and right.

Inscribed in pen and brown ink in upper right corner, *43*.

This sheet of figure studies, no. 99 below, and two other pages at Princeton (48-780 and 48-783) formed part of a sketchbook that must have been broken up in London in the 1920s, shortly before Platt acquired these pages. The drawings were formerly attributed to Sebastiano Ricci, and they do show the strong influence of Ricci's draughtsmanship. But they are demonstrably the work of Fontebasso, whose pen line is broader and coarser, and whose physical types are heavier than Ricci's. The scattered pages of the album, the ruled lines of which suggest that the volume was originally an account book, bear numbers reaching up to fifty-five. Several pages are in the British Museum (1920–9–29-1, 2, and 3 as Fontebasso); there is a page in the Metropolitan Museum (61. 56.2 as Fontebasso), one in the collection of Robert Lehman, another in the collection of David Daniels, New York (repr. *Seventeenth Exhibition of Watercolours and Drawings Presented by John Manning*, London, 1962, no. 74, as Ricci), and eight recently appeared in Paris.

PROVENANCE: Dan Fellows Platt (Lugt 750a), purchased by Platt from Meatyard in London in 1924.

Bequest of Dan Fellows Platt, 48–781

99 *Nude Male Figure, Seen from Behind*

Pen and brown ink, brown and gray wash, over black chalk. 14$\frac{15}{16}$ × 10$\frac{7}{16}$ inches (38 × 26.4 cm.). Vertical ruled lines at left and right. Several spots of brown pigment.

Inscribed in pen and brown ink in upper right corner, *49*.

See no. 98 above.

PROVENANCE: Dan Fellows Platt (Lugt 750a), purchased by Platt from Meatyard in 1924.

Bequest of Dan Fellows Platt, 48–782

GIOVANNI DOMENICO TIEPOLO
Venice 1727 – Venice 1804

100 *Studies of the Virgin, a Prelate, and Other Figures*

Pen and brown ink, brown wash, and red chalk. 10$\frac{1}{4}$ × 11$\frac{1}{16}$ inches (26.1 × 28.1 cm.).

Verso: Pen and brown ink study of a headless draped male figure.

The attribution of this sheet (formerly given to Giambattista) to Domenico Tiepolo is due to J. Byam Shaw, who pointed out that the reclining male figure at the center of the sheet is sketched after the figure of Balthasar Neumann in Giambattista's Europa fresco above the staircase of the Würzburg Residenz (repr. Antonio Morassi, *G. B. Tiepolo. His Life and His Work*, London, 1955, pl. 62). Byam Shaw, who also suggests that the bust of a pope at upper left may be copied after a sculpture by Alessandro Vittoria, dates the sheet about 1753.

PROVENANCE: Dan Fellows Platt (Lugt 750a), purchased by Platt from Naya in 1924.

BIBLIOGRAPHY: Byam Shaw, *Domenico Tiepolo*, p. 72, pl. 6b; Knox, *Princeton Record*, 1964, p. 26, no. 59, repr. p. 18.

Bequest of Dan Fellows Platt, 48–874

101 *Studies of a Seated Prelate*

Reed pen and brown ink. 9$\frac{5}{16}$ × 11$\frac{7}{16}$ inches (23.7 × 29 cm.).

This study for a seated prelate was assigned in the Platt collection to Francesco Guardi, but it is clearly the work of Domenico Tiepolo. Here he has used a broad pen with a freedom comparable to that of the brushwork in no. 100 above.

PROVENANCE: Dan Fellows Platt (Lugt 750a), purchased by Platt from Wheeler in 1937.

Bequest of Dan Fellows Platt, 48–702

102 *Suppliants before the Pope*

Pen and brown ink, brown wash, over a little black chalk. 18⅜×14¼ inches (46.2×36.2 cm.).

Inscribed in pen and brown ink at lower left, *Domo Tiepolo f.*

This drawing is identical in size, technique, and style with a considerable group of drawings, the so-called Biblical Series, by Domenico Tiepolo, representing religious subjects. More than two hundred and fifty of these large, highly finished designs survive. They represent scenes from the Old and New Testaments and perhaps from the Apocryphal Gospels. As Byam Shaw points out, the Princeton sheet, though no doubt part of the series, is unusual in subject, representing as it does a scene from "modern" history. The enthroned pope receiving suppliants is identified as Paul IV Carafa (reigned 1555–1559) by the inscription above his throne.

PROVENANCE: Edward Bergsen (Lugt 827a); Dan Fellows Platt (Lugt 750a), purchased by Platt from Heck in Vienna in 1936.

BIBLIOGRAPHY: Byam Shaw, *Domenico Tiepolo*, p. 36, note 4.

Bequest of Dan Fellows Platt, 48–1289

103 *Physicians Attending a Hypochondriac*

Pen and brown ink, gray-brown wash, over black chalk. 13¹¹⁄₁₆×18¾ inches (34.7 ×47.6 cm.).

The curious headdress with birds' wings worn by one of the doctors also identifies the two medical practitioners in Domenico's Last Illness of Punchinello, a drawing now in the collection of Robert Lehman (Byam Shaw, *Domenico Tiepolo*, pl. 96). The Princeton sheet is not, however, part of the Life of Punchinello series, but rather a satirical drawing inspired by the contemporary Venetian scene.

PROVENANCE: Dan Fellows Platt (Lugt 750a).

BIBLIOGRAPHY: Knox, *Princeton Record*, 1964, p. 28, no. 84, repr. p. 21.

Bequest of Dan Fellows Platt, 48–904

104 *Foreshortened Figures Seated in Clouds*

Pen and brown ink, gray wash. 10½× 7¹¹⁄₁₆ inches (26.7×19.5 cm.). Stains at right margin.

Inscribed in pen and brown ink at lower right, *Dom Tiepolo.*

This signed sheet of figures, and its unsigned companion (no. 105 below) are interesting testimony of just how close the free pen style of Domenico can come to that of his father, Giambattista. Byam Shaw, who dates the present drawing about 1755–1760, points out that the hasty and clumsy drawing of the outstretched arm and hand at the upper right are characteristic of Domenico at this time.

PROVENANCE: Dan Fellows Platt (Lugt 750a), purchased by Platt from Michel in 1933.

BIBLIOGRAPHY: Byam Shaw, *Domenico Tiepolo*, p. 75, pl. 14; Knox, *Princeton Record*, 1964, p. 28, no. 86, repr. p. 21.

Bequest of Dan Fellows Platt, 48–896

105 *Foreshortened Figures Seated in Clouds*

Pen and brown ink, gray wash. $10\frac{7}{16} \times 7\frac{3}{4}$ inches (26.5 × 19.7 cm.).

See no. 104 above.

PROVENANCE: Dan Fellows Platt (Lugt 750a), purchased by Platt from Michel in 1933.

BIBLIOGRAPHY: Knox, *Princeton Record*, 1964, p. 28, no. 87, repr. p. 21.

Bequest of Dan Fellows Platt, 48–906

UBALDO GANDOLFI
S. Matteo della Decima 1728 – Ravenna 1781

106 *St. Dominic*

Pen and brown ink, gray and a little red wash. $14\frac{13}{16} \times 9$ inches (37.6 × 22.9 cm.). Lined.

Inscribed on verso of old mount in black pencil, *B. Strozzi*.

This drawing entered the Princeton inventory under the name of Bernardo Strozzi; the erroneous attribution is presumably based on an inscription on the old mount. The sheet is instead a good example of the draughtsmanship of Ubaldo Gandolfi. It is rather difficult to make a clear-cut distinction between the pen drawing styles of Ubaldo and of his younger brother Gaetano (1734–1802), but the Princeton sheet is strikingly similar to drawings traditionally ascribed to Ubaldo (for example, three sheets in the Albertina, repr. A. Stix and A. Spitzmüller, *Beschreibender Katalog der Handzeichnungen in der Staatlichen Graphischen Sammlung Albertina*, VI, *Die Schulen von Ferrara, Bologna,* . . ., Vienna, 1941, nos. 326, 327, and 328).

PROVENANCE: Dan Fellows Platt (Lugt 750a).

Bequest of Dan Fellows Platt, 48–825

INDEX OF ARTISTS

LIST OF PLATES

69. G. B. GAULLI, attributed to, The Flood

70. DONATO CRETI, Studies for Jacob Wrestling with the Angel

71. MARCO RICCI, Pilgrims Resting

72. ALESSANDRO MAGNASCO, Penitent Monk

73. G. B. PIAZZETTA, Head of a Woman

74. GASPARO DIZIANI, Apollo and Marsyas

75. G. B. TIEPOLO, Soldier

76. G. B. TIEPOLO, Faith, Hope, and Charity

77. G. B. TIEPOLO, Prudence and a River God

78. G. B. TIEPOLO, Male and Female Fauns

79. G. B. TIEPOLO, Seated Virgin and Child

80. G. B. TIEPOLO, St. Paulinus Exorcising a Possessed Boy

81. G. B. TIEPOLO, St. Paulinus Exorcising a Possessed Boy

82. G. B. TIEPOLO, St. Paulinus Exorcising a Possessed Boy

83. G. B. TIEPOLO, Roger Mounted on a Hippogriff

84. G. B. TIEPOLO, Study for Faith, Hope, and Charity

85. G. B. TIEPOLO, Head, after a Bust of Palma Giovane by Alessandro Vittoria

86. G. B. TIEPOLO, Walking Man, Back View

87. G. B. TIEPOLO, Man in Turban

88. G. B. TIEPOLO, Standing Man, Frontal

89. G. B. TIEPOLO, Woman Holding Platter

90. G. B. TIEPOLO, Seated Figure, Arms Raised

91. G. B. TIEPOLO, Seated Figure, Hand to Head

92. G. B. TIEPOLO, Reclining Youth with Staff

93. G. B. TIEPOLO, Figure Striding, Holding Knee

94. G. B. TIEPOLO, Female Figure, Right Arm Raised

95. G. B. TIEPOLO, Male Head, Profile to Left

96. POMPEO BATONI, Sleeping Christ Child

97. FRANCESCO FONTEBASSO, Nymphs in a Landscape

98. FRANCESCO FONTEBASSO, Studies of Nude Male Figures

99. FRANCESCO FONTEBASSO, Nude Male Figure Seen from Behind

100. DOMENICO TIEPOLO, Studies of the Virgin, a Prelate, and Other Figures

101. DOMENICO TIEPOLO, Studies of a Seated Prelate

102. DOMENICO TIEPOLO, Suppliants before the Pope

103. DOMENICO TIEPOLO, Physicians Attending a Hypochondriac

104. DOMENICO TIEPOLO, Foreshortened Figures Seated in Clouds

105. DOMENICO TIEPOLO, Foreshortened Figures Seated in Clouds

106. UBALDO GANDOLFI, St. Dominic

PLATES

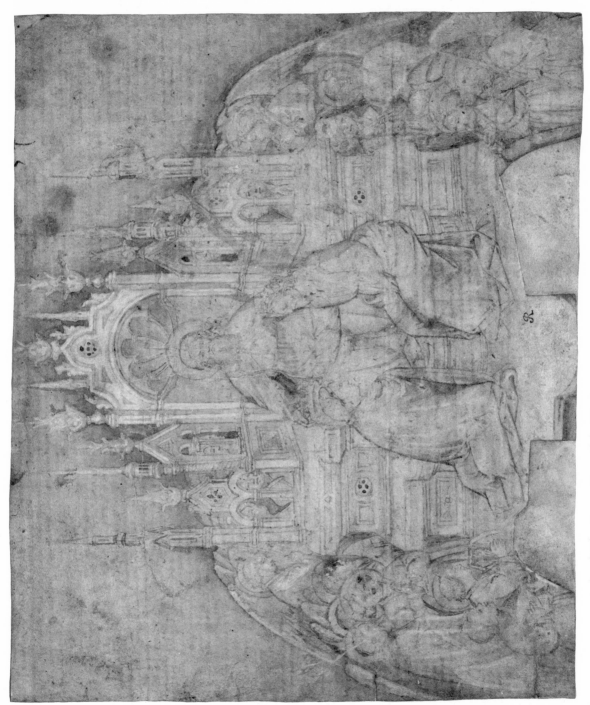

I. ALTICHIERO, circle of, The Coronation of the Virgin

2. VITTORE CARPACCIO, Two Standing Female Figures

2 (verso). VITTORE CARPACCIO, Head of a Man and Head of a Lion

3. DOMENICO BECCAFUMI, Head of a Woman

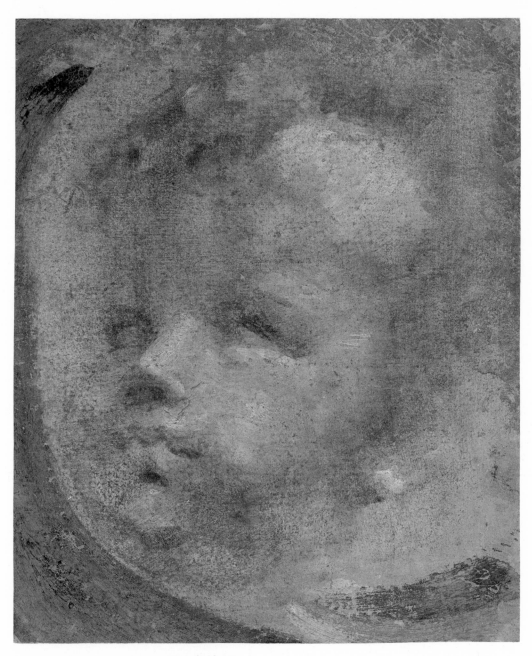

4. DOMENICO BECCAFUMI, Head of a Putto

5. DOMENICO BECCAFUMI, Scene from the Life of St. Anthony Abbot

6. RAPHAEL, school of, A Papal Audience

7. GIULIO ROMANO, Man Beating a Snarling Dog

8. PERINO DEL VAGA, studio of, Kneeling Figure of Mercury

9. PARMIGIANINO, Seated Figure with Goats

IO. LELI

11. JACOPO TINTORETTO, Study of a Nude Male Figure

12. ANDREA SCHIAVONE, The Adoration of the Shepherds

13. FEDERICO BAROCCI, Figure Studies

14. FEDERICO BAROCCI, Study of a Torso

15. FEDERICO BAROCCI, Studies of Legs

16. LUCA CAMBIASO, The Conversion of St. Paul

17. LUCA CAMBIASO, The Return of Ulysses

18. GIROLAMO MACCHIETTI, Seated Male Nude

19. BATTISTA NALDINI, Copy after Michelangelo's Giuliano de' Medici

20. BATTISTA NALDINI, Copy after Michelangelo's Lorenzo de' Medici

21. FEDERICO ZUCCARO, Studies of the Head of a Bearded Man

22. JACOPO ZUCCHI, The Age of Gold

23. JACOPO BERTOIA, Studies for a Seated Virgin and Child, and Other Figures

23 (verso). JACOPO BERTOIA, Studies of Putti, a Cartouche, and Two Heads

24. PALMA GIOVANE, The Virgin and Child Appearing to Five Saints

25. PALMA GIOVANE, Back View of a Nude Male Figure

26. ANDREA BOSCOLI, Frieze of Figures Bearing Offerings

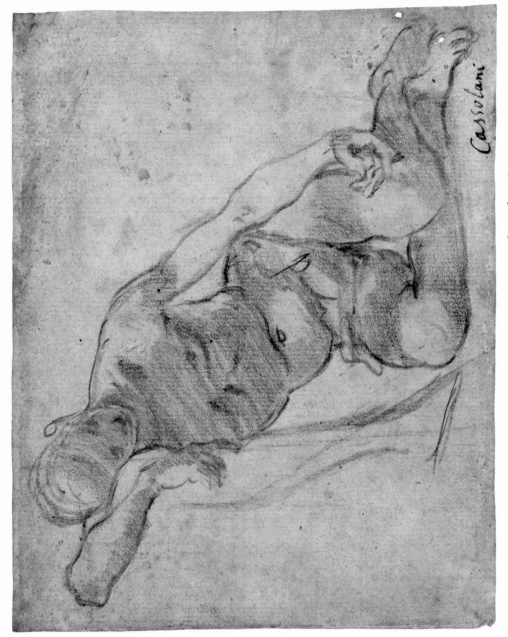

27. ALESSANDRO CASOLANI, Nude Youth Resting Against the Leg of Another Figure

28. ANNIBALE CARRACCI, Portrait of a Young Man

29. DOMENICO TINTORETTO, The Virgin Interceding before Christ
for Plague-Stricken Venice

30. DOMENICO TINTORETTO, The Adoration of the Shepherds

31. FERRAÙ FENZONI, The Massacre of the Innocents

32. REMIGIO CANTAGALLINA, View of a Village Square and Church

33. MARCANTONIO BASSETTI, The Martyrdom of the Ten Thousand

34. GUERCINO, Madonna and Child with St. Anthony of Padua

35. GUERCINO, A Couple Conversing

36. GUERCINO, The Arrest of Christ

37. GUERCINO, Kneeling Penitent Saint

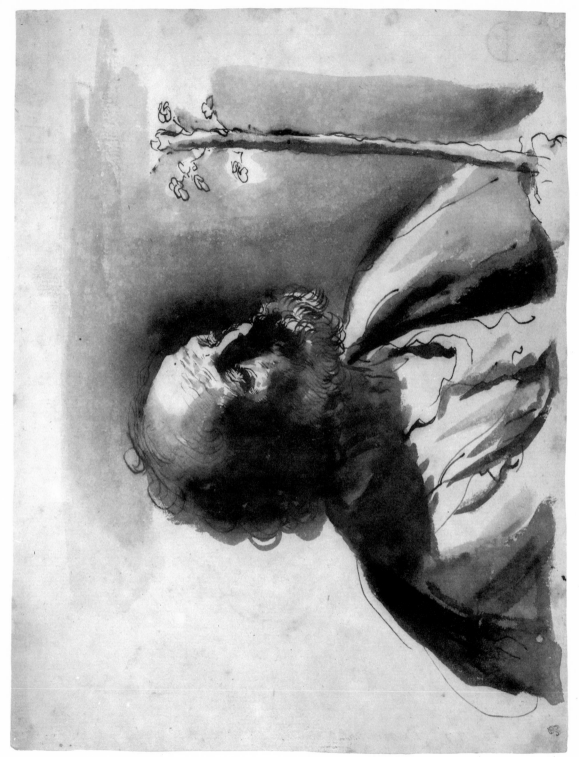

38. GUERCINO, Half Figure of St. Joseph Holding a Staff

39. GUERCINO, The Visitation

40. GUERCINO, The Martyrdom of St. Bartholomew

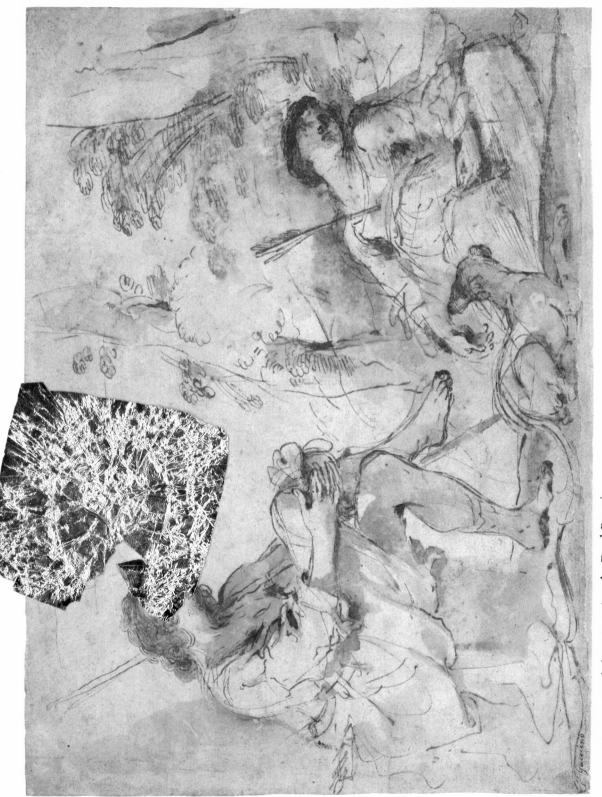

41. GUERCINO, Cephalus Mourning the Dead Procris

42. GUERCINO, Head of a Bearded Man Looking Down

43. GUERCINO, Profile of a Man Facing Right

44. GUERCINO, Head of a Pope

45. GUERCINO, Caricature of a Boy Wearing a Broad-Brimmed Hat

46. GUERCINO, Caricature of a Woman with Deformed Lips

47. GUERCINO, Caricature of a Man in a Cap with Hands Crossed on His Chest

48. GUERCINO, Veronica's Veil Imprinted with the Face of Christ

49. GUERCINO, copy after, Veronica's Veil

50. PIETRO DA CORTONA, Study for the Age of Iron

51. G. B. CASTIGLIONE, Joseph Interpreting Dreams

52. FRANCESCO MONTELATICI, Reclining Youth

53. PIER FRANCESCO MOLA, The Flight into Egypt

54. PIER FRANCESCO MOLA, Joseph Interpreting Dreams

55. PIER FRANCESCO MOLA, Studies for the Penitent St. Jerome

56. SALVATOR ROSA, Studies for a Witches' Sabbath

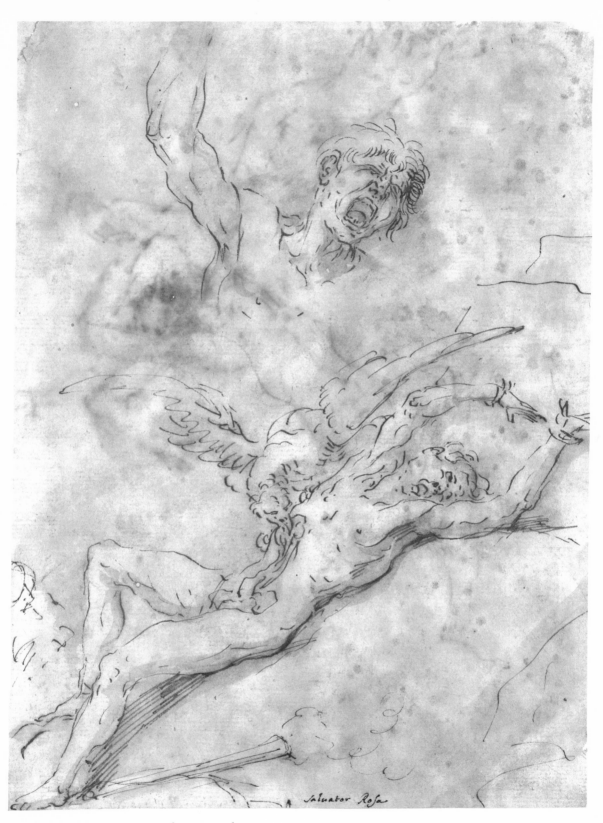

57. SALVATOR ROSA, Prometheus Bound

58. SALVATOR ROSA, Studies for the Death of Regulus

59. SALVATOR ROSA, The Adoration of the Shepherds

60. SALVATOR ROSA, Kneeling Figures

61. SALVATOR ROSA, Studies of a Male Figure with Right Arm Raised, and of a
Kneeling Female Figure

62. SALVATOR ROSA, Studies of an Executioner

63. SALVATOR ROSA, Youth Pulling
off His Shirt, Full Figure

64. SALVATOR ROSA, Youth Pulling
off His Shirt, Half Figure

65. DOMENICO PIOLA, Three Seated Female Figures, Two Putti, and a Dog

66. DOMENICO PIOLA, Madonna and Child with the Infant Baptist

67. CIRO FERRI, The Martyrdom of St. Bibiana

68. CESARE GENNARI, Caricature of a Man in a Turban Holding a Pestle

69. G. B. GAULLI, attributed to, The Flood

70. DONATO CRETI, Studies for Jacob Wrestling with the Angel

71. **MARCO RICCI**; Pilgrims Resting

72. ALESSANDRO MAGNASCO, Penitent Monk

73. G. B. PIAZZETTA, Head of a Woman

74. GASPARO DIZIANI, Apollo and Marsyas

75. G. B. TIEPOLO, Soldier

76. G. B. TIEPOLO, Faith, Hope, and Charity

77. G. B. TIEPOLO, Prudence and a River God

78. G. B. TIEPOLO, Male and Female Fauns

79. G. B. TIEPOLO, Seated Virgin and Child

80. G. B. TIEPOLO, St. Paulinus Exorcising a Possessed Boy

81. G. B. TIEPOLO, St. Paulinus Exorcising a Possessed Boy

82. G. B. TIEPOLO, St. Paulinus Exorcising a Possessed Boy

83. G. B. TIEPOLO, Roger Mounted on a Hippogriff

84. G. B. TIEPOLO, Study for Faith, Hope, and Charity

85. G. B. TIEPOLO, Head, after a Bust of Palma Giovane by Alessandro Vittoria

86. G. B. TIEPOLO, Walking Man, Back View

87. G. B. TIEPOLO, Man in Turban

88. G. B. TIEPOLO, Standing Man, Frontal

109

89. G. B. TIEPOLO, Woman Holding Platter

90. G. B. TIEPOLO, Seated Figure, Arms Raised

91. G. B. TIEPOLO, Seated Figure, Hand to Head

92. G. B. TIEPOLO, Reclining Youth with Staff

93. G. B. TIEPOLO, Figure Striding, Holding Knee

94. G. B. TIEPOLO, Female Figure, Right Arm Raised

95. G. B. TIEPOLO, Male Head, Profile to Left

96. POMPEO BATONI, Sleeping Christ Child

97. FRANCESCO FONTEBASSO, Nymphs in a Landscape

98. FRANCESCO FONTEBASSO, Studies of Nude Male Figures

99. FRANCESCO FONTEBASSO, Nude Male Figure Seen from Behind

100. DOMENICO TIEPOLO, Studies of the Virgin, a Prelate, and Other Figures

IOI. DOMENICO TIEPOLO, Studies of a Seated Prelate

102. DOMENICO TIEPOLO, Suppliants before the Pope

103. DOMENICO TIEPOLO, Physicians Attending a Hypochondriac

104. DOMENICO TIEPOLO, Foreshortened Figures Seated in Clouds

105. DOMENICO TIEPOLO, Foreshortened Figures Seated in Clouds

106. UBALDO GANDOLFI, St. Dominic